G000271633

ROVER
SGL LEYLAND
PRESTON ROAD, LEYLAND
LANCASHIRE. PR5 2NT
Telephone: 0772 452311

ROVER

THE FIRST NINETY YEARS

One of Britain's Fine Cars

ROVER

THE FIRST NINETY YEARS

1904 ◆ 1994

Eric Dymock

DOVE PUBLISHING

First published in Great Britain in 1993 by
DOVE PUBLISHING
Old Chapel House, Sutton Veny, Wiltshire BA12 7AY

Text copyright © Eric Dymock 1993
Commissioned colour photography © Sandy Porter

Designed by Ruth Dymock with
Andrew Barron & Collis Clements Associates

All rights reserved. No part of this publication may be
reproduced, stored in a retrieval system, or transmitted in any
form or by any means, electronic, mechanical, photocopying,
recording or otherwise, without the prior permission of the
copyright holder

British Library Cataloguing-in-Publication Data. A catalogue
record for this book is available from the British Library

ISBN 0 9518750 1 9

Electronic processing by Manuscript

Colour separation by Fotographics Ltd,
London and Hong Kong

Made and printed in Great Britain by
Butler and Tanner Ltd, Frome

Contents

One of Britain's Fine Cars

By roads 'not adopted' by woodlanded ways,
She drove to the club in the late summer haze,
Into nine o'clock Camberley, heavy with bells
And mushroomy, pine-woody, evergreen smells.

Around us are Rovers and Austins afar,
Above us the intimate roof of the car...

from: *A Subaltern's Love Song*
by John Betjeman

Ellis's cycle shop in
Salop Road, Oswestry
before the turn of the
century. Rival
advertisements for
Sunbeam, Humber,
Singer and
Rudge-Whitworth cycles.
(left)

R over cars did not have the stuff of adventure about them until the 1930s. The hesitant beginners of 1904 were sturdy and innovative, the tall Edwardians had a certain dignity, and those of the 1920s showed flair. Yet perversely it was not until the dark days of the Depression that the Light Six and the Meteor, then the Pilot and the car that came to be known as the P1, created the mould in which Rover's reputation would be cast.

They were years of crisis. Rover came of age amid the growing power of European dictators and the plight of the abdication. None the less, the burgeoning British middle class somehow came to regard a Rover as a sign of continuity and dependability.

Rovers symbolised good taste and embraced qualities that caught the nation's mood. They were certainly among the best cars of the day. One of Britain's Fine Cars was an evocative slogan describing a vehicle so distinctive in character and culture that John Betjeman could use it to evoke a way of life.

Rover began with the radical backbone-framed pioneer designs of Edmund Lewis in 1904, carrying on right up to the threshold of the 21st century, with computer-aided designs from a world-wide staff. The early technology was rooted in the 19th-century West Midlands bicycle industry, and began a dynasty that stretched over ninety years to world-class vehicles in numbers that the Edwardian pioneers could scarcely imagine. Here was a name from the industrial heart of Britain that gave a hallmark to the world.

Rover was still making bicycles when much of the Midlands motor industry was getting into gear. It marked itself out for distinction early, with two flashes of genius that showed its flair for innovation and an aptitude for identifying a distinctive clientele.

The aptitude proved enduring. The technical quality of the engineering was good, but the Midlands businessmen running the company endowed Rover with a rare talent for matching its products to its customers. It knew its resources; it always knew

Edwardian magnificence.
Strength was the keynote
of the tall wheels
of the 1912 12hp
landaulette.
(above)

THE "ROVER.

BRADLEY BIRM.ᵍ

THE POPULAR MACHINE FOR 1884.

what it was best at. Its skill lay in building the right car for its market.

The talent was knowing what a prosperous swathe of the British middle-class wanted to drive. A knack for engineering was needed to carry it through. It meant knowing the customer, and making what he wanted

with unwavering precision. In the end it meant knowing as much about people as about cars.

There were times when the concept nearly failed. The proliferation of models in the late 1920s nearly bankrupt the company. The shortage of wealthy customers following the

wars of 1914-1918 and 1939-1945 brought crises of different sorts.

Yet resourcefulness such as that shown by John Kemp Starley in the 1880s saw Rover through. The founder had a rare faculty for identifying the consumer, deciding what he wanted then making it. Born in Walthamstow in 1855, Starley joined his uncle James making bicycles in Coventry, inventing among other things a device called a Coventry chair, like a Bath chair moved by pedalling.

The first touch of genius was Starley's. In 1886 he made other bicycles out of date almost overnight. The Starley safety cycle had a diamond-shaped frame, a brake operated from the handlebar, and a geared-up chain drive to the back wheel.

Starley's conviction that the rear wheel of a bicycle should be driven was critical. For the first time the gearing of the chain sprockets allowed a bicycle two equal-sized wheels. The old precarious 'Ordinary', the penny-farthing with the pedals in the middle of the tall front wheel, was rendered obsolete, and a landmark reached in the history of transportation.

It did not look like a landmark at the time. Starley's invention was derided as unmanly. Its superiority soon became apparent when George Smith knocked five minutes off the British 100 miles record. The Imperial Rover

The first Rover was laboriously propelled by hand and foot.
The 1884 tricycle.
(left)

An endorsement by the president of the National Cyclists Union was used for a Special Rover with sprung frame and chain drive.
(right)

THE

'Special Rover' Bicycle.

(Patented and Registered.)

As ridden by the
RIGHT HON.
VISCOUNT BURY,
President of
the National Cyclists'
Union

Chainless Lady's Rover

SPECIFICATION.

Frame— 22-in., 24-in., or 26-in.

Forks—Box crown, oval to round sides, 3½-in. curve; lamp bracket.

Handle-bar—Upturned, celluloid handles.

Saddle—Brooks' B302L, plated springs.

Tool-bag—Brooks' No. 9060/1, with cleaning cloth and tools.

Gear—63-in.

Cranks—"Rover" pattern, 6½-in.

Pedals— 3¼-in. 'Rover' pattern, rubber.

Wheels— 28-in., black enamelled centres, lined to match frame, plated tracks.

Tyres— 1½-in. Dunlops.

Spokes—Double butted, of the highest possible quality, enamelled black, plated centres.

Guards— Best steel, with strengthened edges; extension to front guard, rear guard laced for the protection of the dress.

Brakes—Coaster hub and front rim brake, or two rim brakes with free wheel.

Steering—Special ball-bearings top and bottom; "Rover" steering lock.

Bearings—All cups, cones, and balls of special steel.

Finish—Finest quality black enamel, fine bronze lines, with centre line green, all bright parts heavily plated on copper

proved itself the best in the world by winning every race in the 1908 Olympic Games.

The Rover safety bicycle was copied across the globe, and more than a century later modern cycles and mountain bikes faithfully observed its pattern. It was as much of a milestone as Karl Benz's contemporaneous car and the Wright brothers' 1903 Flyer.

The Rover Safety inaugurated the commercial, practical bicycle, and even the Lotus Olympic racing machine of the 1990s followed the prototype proportions of Starley's in the 1880s. 'Rover' was coined for a tricycle advertised as suitable for 'roving' in 1884 and Rover continued making bicycles that never entirely lost the pioneering spirit. The last ones, with a brake operated by pedalling

anticlockwise, endowed the English language with 'back-pedalling', meaning to check a movement or reverse an action.

Rover's second stroke of genius came in 1888. Gottlieb Daimler and Wilhelm Maybach completed their first petrol carriage in 1886, and Karl Benz ran his through the streets of Mannheim, just as Starley began work on the first Rover automobile. This was an electric car completed sixteen years before Rover's first production petrol car of 1904.

It was recalled in a 1903 issue of *The Autocar*: '*This was, we believe, the first motor machine made in Coventry. It was produced at the Meteor works in West Orchard Street in 1888 by the late Mr J K Starley of Starley & Sutton (the introducer of the modern or rear-driving or safety bicycle) whose name is so well known in connection with the Rover make. The little car was driven by electricity, the motor and accumulators being supplied by Mr Edwell of Messrs Edwell Parker Ltd, Wolverhampton. The body was made by Messrs Hollick who still do much motor car coachwork. It will be seen that the steering was effected through a spade handle and pinion working on a toothed quadrant. As Mr Starley found that he was not allowed by law to drive the machine in England at more than 4mph on the roads, and not even at that speed unless it was preceded by a man with a red flag, he took it over*

Chainless wonder. Shaft-drive ladies bicycle developed by Rover to avoid danger of long skirts tangling with oily chain. (left)

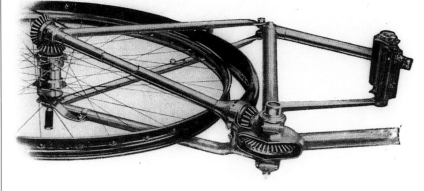

Ingenious gear-driven
shaft to rear wheel of
Rover's ladies bicycle.
(above right)

John Kemp Starley, the
founding father who never
lived to see the Rover car
in production.
(below)

THE LATE
MR. JOHN KEMP STARLEY,
The introducer of the "Rover" Bicycle, the pioneer of
the present-day cycle.

*to France and tested it at Deauville, a
place which has since become famous
for its motor races.*

*'It gave every satisfaction and
averaged about 8mph. We are indebted
to Mr Harry Smith, managing director
of the Rover Cycle Company, for the
very interesting photograph and
particulars concerning it.'*

The 1888 electric Rover, like Starley's
Coventry chair, seemed also to draw
inspiration from the Bath chair.
It had two large rear wheels and a
small one in front guided by a tiller.
The sofa-like two-seater chair had a
rounded back with wooden rails, and
the motor was below the rear axle,
with a wicker hamper above it
containing the batteries. It was little
more than an exploration of
mechanical wheeled transport, and it
is unlikely any were ever sold.
Its range was poor and it was too
heavy to pedal.

Starley prospered in the bicycle boom
of the 1890s, married the daughter of a
Coventry ribbon manufacturer, and
had ten children. Like his uncle James,
who had a statue dedicated to him in
Warwick Row, Coventry, J K became
a prominent citizen. He supported the
Salvation Army, became a Liberal
member of the city council and
president of the YMCA, and had
special versions of the Bible printed,
known as the Starley Bible, in which
the New Testament came first.

In 1896 J K Starley & Co became the
Rover Cycle Company, went public,
and Starley collected £100,000.

Rover was the largest cycle works in
Coventry, and Starley imported
Peugeot motorcycles but
unaccountably lost his nerve following
a downturn in the cycle market in
1897. He tried to run down the
company until the crisis was over, but
his health failed and he died in 1901
at the age of 46.

Harry Smith took over as managing
director, Frank Ward as company
secretary, and young Jack Starley
became assistant works manager.
Together they carried on with
the introduction of a fore-car,
a tricycle with a wicker-basket chair
between the two front wheels. It cost
£65 with three wheels, £55 as a plain
motorcycle. It had a four-stroke
$2\frac{1}{4}$hp engine with an automatic
overhead inlet valve, cam-operated side
exhaust valve, and spray-type
carburettor.

There was no gearbox or clutch, it was
driven by a permanently engaged belt,
and started by pedalling off with the
exhaust valve held open. Once it was
moving, closing the valve was
supposed to make the engine fire.
Smith was more optimistic than the
sickly Starley. His response to sluggish
bicycle sales was to start making cars.

Rover entered the market in 1904, and
unlike many of its rivals chose not to
plagiarise a design from abroad.
Two years after Starley's death, in
December 1903, the company tempted
Edmund Lewis to leave Daimler and
take it into a new era.

Lewis aimed for the mass market.
Rover had been successful making
large numbers of bicycles, and Harry
Smith saw no reason why it should not
make large numbers of cars.

Progress was swift, although Lewis
had to reintroduce a less radical Rover
to replace his first adventurous design.
Later production versions were more

successful, and a Rover won the Isle of Man Tourist Trophy race in 1907. Lewis's radicalism was not forgotten, and in 1911 Rover flirted with the sleeve-valve engine designed by the American Charles J Knight.

Commercially the Knight cars were not a success. Dudley Noble, later director of publicity and a distinguished journalist, joined Rover in 1911 as a motorcycle tester and found things in bad shape. He thought the sleeve-valve cars 'a decided flop'.

Years later Noble revealed how Rover was investigating other engines besides the sleeve-valve. In September 1913 he was dispatched with a 12hp to Harwich to meet the celebrated Dr Rudolph Diesel off the overnight ferry from Antwerp. Noble had photographs of Diesel, a letter of introduction, and instructions to bring him to Coventry as soon as he disembarked.

He waited in the cold light of an autumn dawn, at the Harwich customs shed, in vain. Dr Diesel had been on the cross-Channel packet 'SS Dresden', but his cabin was empty, his bed had not been slept in and he was presumed lost overboard.

Diesel's engine had applications beyond those Rover had in mind. It was of profound strategic importance for submarines, and both the British Admiralty and the Kaiser's navy were

interested in the plans contained in the briefcase that vanished with him.

Rover got no further with diesel engines for another twenty years, and it was the 1980s before a Rover saloon car was equipped with one. It was the orthodox poppet-valve petrol engines of the Edwardian era that turned out worthy, strong and reliable. Designed by Owen Clegg, another of the robust personalities who punctuated Rover history, these included a 2.3-litre four-cylinder 12hp, shown at Olympia in 1912. Clegg's brilliant design, which helped Rover into its own particular niche in the quality market, sold for £350 and survived the war as the Rover Fourteen.

Sales soared from 883 in 1911 to 1,943 in 1914, profits increased, and by 1912 Rover had a substantial selection of vehicles ranging from bicycles between £6 10s and £15 2s 6d, motorcycles from £49 to £79, and cars from 100 guineas to 600 guineas. During the war, Rover failed to obtain War Office contracts for staff cars, unlike Crossley Sunbeam and Vauxhall.

Instead Rover built staff car and ambulance bodies on the Sunbeam 12/16 chassis, and Maudslay lorries. It enriched itself as the war dragged on making mortars, gas shells, fuses and components for tanks as well as Rover cycles and military motorcycles. In the end it needed more space and leased another factory in Helen Street,

Coventry, where it completed 1,781 Sunbeams, probably more than Sunbeam could have managed, and 500 Maudslays.

Rover came back to cars after the war, with the Rover Eight at £300, and acquired another factory at Tyseley, Birmingham, to make it. Competition was fierce; the Eight's price was whittled down to £160 and production steadily increased. Between 1920 and 1925, 40,000 were made, and a further 17,000 under licence in Germany by Peter und Moritz.

The Eight was a novel air-cooled flat twin, with cylinder heads that stuck out into the airstream. It was not a very fast airstream - 45mph on a good day - so the tiny engine overheated and the cylinder heads glowed in the dark. Cheerful and cheap, it never enjoyed the success of the Austin Seven, and as the 1920s progressed Rover turned back to its supporters among the better-off.

It was still out of luck. It introduced an overhead camshaft engine in 1925 that was technically adept, but commercially unsuccessful, in a rather slow and heavy car. Rovers, however praiseworthy, still tended to be unexciting.

The 9/20 was an overhead-valve, water-cooled, in-line four, listed at £215. It was provided with front-wheel brakes in 1926, and in 1927 a

1905 Rover 8hp.
Sketchy bodywork and large aluminium castings characterised Edmund Lewis's early Rovers.
(left)

Certificate of Agency.

"THE ROVER HAS SET THE FASHION TO THE WORLD"
"THE CYCLIST."

The Rover Cycle Co., Limited,
LATE
J.K. Starley & Co. Limited,
Meteor Works, West Orchard,
Coventry. England.

SOLE MAKERS OF THE
ROVER BICYCLE & COVENTRY CHAIR.

This is to Certify that we have given
Messrs G & H Ellis
Salop Rd Oswestry
the sole right to sell our Rover Cycles in
Oswestry and district
for the Season ending October 31st 1897
subject to the conditions set forth in our letter
confirming the appointment.

Dated this 1st day of November 1896

The Rover Cycle Co., Limited,
LATE
J.K. Starley & Co Limited.

pioneering detachable hard-top coupé body. Rover won the RAC Dewar Trophy with a 14/45 for fifty ascents of Bwlch-y-Groes, a steep, winding hill in Wales, at a time when getting to the top at all was something of an achievement.

The 1920s saw the adoption of the helmeted Viking and the triangular badge that intrigued generations of owners. It began as an innocent pun on the most famous rovers of all - the Vikings. A shield was a convenient shape to go on the front upright of a bicycle, and from 1902 a motorcycle.

The radiator shape evolved from a shield to a rectangle, still with cut-outs on the shoulders, with the 12hp in 1912. In 1922 owners were offered a mascot for the radiator filler cap as an optional extra for £1.

Mascots or talismans were popular accessories, and Rover embraced the Viking, complete with winged helmet, battleaxe and shield. Hispano-Suiza went for a stork, Armstrong-Siddeley a sphinx, and Rolls-Royce the famous Spirit of Ecstasy. Other makes had greyhounds, flying fish, birds, animals and voluptuous nymphs.

Rover's upstanding Viking gave way in due course to his head alone, still with helmet, then logically enough this became the figurehead of a Viking longship. The Viking ship prow and sail first appeared on a radiator badge in 1929, and evolved with curving bow-wave symbolically throughout Rover history. The biggest Viking badge appeared on the Rover 2000 of 1963 as the centrepiece of the grille.

First to wear the Viking head mascot, and the enamel badge of black longship ploughing through blue seas, was

Rover dealer agreement for 1897 with G & H Ellis of Oswestry, Shropshire. (left)

a 2-litre saloon in 1930. One of these, a Light Six, carried the distinctive heraldry when it raced the Blue Train through France.

It was a moderately shameless stunt by Dudley Noble, safe in the knowledge that the average speed of the famous express was no more than about 40mph once all its stops and detours were taken into account. To beat it, Noble had to drive more or less non-stop from Calais to the Riviera.

He defeated the train after two false starts, but at the third attempt his crew became celebrities through the *Daily Express*. The Light Six did well out of it, but the incoming management felt it undignified and Rover publicity was gently redrawn to accommodate customers' delicate tastes. Rover never overlooked its buyers: their tastes were its tastes, their aspiration its aspirations. They were never forgotten.

Noble's bright idea illuminated Rover's success. A vigorous new management turned it from a pioneer into a pillar of the establishment. The tough economic climate of the late 1920s brought it to the verge of collapse in the early 1930s. The shareholders had been paid no dividend since 1923, and although Rover cars were well received, a good name was not enough. A shareholders' action committee was formed.

It was time for something more than a

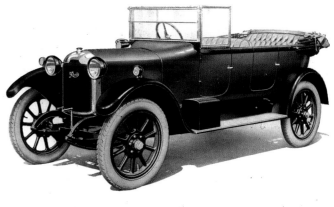

ROVER

SPECIFICATION

ENGINE. — Four cylinder, monobloc, water-cooled, side-by-side valves. Cylinders are offset, and have detachable heads. Oil pumped under pressure to all bearings and big-ends by mechanical pump located at bottom of sump. Sump has capacity for approx. 1½ gallons of oil. Magneto and cam-shafts driven by silent chains. Water-cooling by pump.
Bore of cylinders, 75 mm. (2.952 ins.).
Stroke of pistons, 130 mm. (5.11 ins.).
Capacity of engine, 2,296 c.c. (140 cu. ins.).

CLUTCH. — Metal to metal, running in oil. Single plate type.

GEARS — Four speeds forward and reverse. Gate change. Direct drive on top gear. Ratios: 5.14, 8.4, 13.3 and 21.4 to 1. Reverse 18.2 to 1. (Reverse only in motion when in use).

SPRINGS.—Special high grade steel, enclosed in leather gaiters. Volute buffer springs fitted on front axle to save jarring on bad pot-holes.

IGNITION.—Lucas magneto; control lever on steering wheel.

PETROL TANK.—Capacity: 13½ gallons. Car-ried at rear of chassis. Vacuum feed to carburetter.

WHEELS. — Pressed steel, quickly detachable. Two spares provided.

TYRES.—Heavy Dunlop cords, straight sided, including spare wheels.
Size: 815 mm. x 105 mm. (32 ins. x 4 ins.).

BODY.—Streamline type, to seat four or five. Fitted with mats back and front. Nickel finish. Pockets in all doors. Choice of finish.

TOOL KIT.—Containing complete tool equip-ment. Carried in pockets of rear doors.

LIGHTING. — Rotax 12-volt set, separate dynamo. Two head, two side, and tail lamps, also dash lamp.

HOOD.—One-man type, spring lift. Clamps to top of screen. Fitted with all-weather side curtains (which are carried behind front seat when not in use). Side curtains open with door, and can be left in position when hood is not raised, thus giving protection to pas-sengers in rear seat. An interior electric light is provided, also a hood cover.

SCREEN. — Fixed metal sides to meet hood. Both halves of screen adjustable.

STARTER.—Electrical, geared with flywheel. Operated by push button on dash.

SPEEDOMETER. — Flush fitting on dash. Best quality.

CLOCK.—Flush fitting on dash. Best quality.

HORNS.—Both electric and bulb horns are fitted as standard.

LUGGAGE GRID. – Fitted at rear end of chassis. Complete with straps.

DIMENSIONS.—

Wheelbase	...	...	9 ft. 8 ins.
Overall width	...	...	6 ft. 2 ins.
Weight complete	...	...	26 cwt. approx.
Track	...	...	4 ft. 8½ ins.
Overall length	...	...	13 ft. 8 ins.
Height (hood up)	...	...	6 ft. 7 ins.

change. A transformation had to be wrought, and it fell to Spencer Wilks and his brother Maurice to provide Rover with a new lease of life. Spencer Bernau Wilks was born in

Rickmansworth, came from a wealthy family, and trained as a barrister before enlisting in the army in 1914. He joined Hillman in 1919, made a success of it as managing director in

Advertising for the 'Clegg Twelve' in 1923 featured the post-war improvements to the design. Prices were from £550. (right)

the 1920s, and married one of William Hillman's six daughters.

He left following the Rootes takeover in 1928, and became works manager at Rover when the firm was losing £2,000 to £3,000 a week and Lloyds Bank limited its overdraft to £235,000. Two principal creditors, Lucas and Pressed Steel, installed H Howe Graham as

managing director and a boardroom revolution brought the appointment of a former tank corps commander, Colonel Frank Searle, to run the company.

Rover had lost its way. It had no strong identity such as Riley, Sunbeam, Lanchester, Wolseley or Lea-Francis had. Inefficiency, indifferent cars, unreliability and poor forecasting led to a financial haemorrhage that the shareholders were no longer prepared to put up with.

Rover made fewer cars at the end of the 1920s than it had at the start, and its share of a market that had grown four-fold, slumped from a healthy 9 per cent to a niggardly 2.3 per cent.

Searle did not know much about the motor industry, but he could see the need for leadership. In September 1929 he recruited Spencer Wilks to administer the swift surgery that was needed. It took Wilks until the 1931 model year to put things right, turning the company round by an astute combination of good management, secure engineering and a feel for what the customers wanted to drive. The range was rationalised, new designs put in hand and a realistic policy adopted that suited a company Rover's size.

Sir Alfred Mays-Smith, a powerful board director, considered Searle no more than a caretaker and promptly

The heart-shaped radiator of 1907 20hp. Name-plate bogus; it was added later to enhance identification. (below)

Carriage for Edwardian nobility and gentry. (right)

made Wilks his successor. He hastened the departure of Peter Poppe, the engineer whose cars had been technically engaging but unsuccessful.

Wilks intuitively knew what to do. He instituted a range of cars that quickly inspired the affection of Britain's new middle class. It was another flash of inspiration that matched Rovers to their clients. Rovers became something more than mere cars. They represented a style of life, something as comfortable as a fireside chat or a picnic in the country. They epitomised good taste, good value, staunch tradition, a style the passing of which would be mourned, at the end of the 1930s by Betjeman's subaltern.

Rover moved away from the genteel but declining grandeur of limousines furnished like small railway carriages and driven by chauffeurs. Rovers became refined cars for owners who drove themselves but still preserved some middle-class seemliness. To this post-Depression bourgeoisie, the cars had the lustre of small Rolls-Royces. Rovers were quiet and refined, with a sense of propriety - solemnity almost - and embodied good, sound, reliable engineering.

It took time to turn the company round financially. A year after Wilks joined, things looked as bad as ever, with large numbers of cars unsold and an annual loss of £80,000. At the end of 1931 Searle was sent to visit dealers in

New Zealand (the antipodes were unsafe for Rover executives - Jack Starley, grandson of the founder, was exiled in Australia) and Wilks found himself given a free hand.

H Howe Graham was first appointed financial director by a jittery Lloyds Bank, then a consultant. He was able to return to the board of directors only when Rover's recovery gathered speed in 1934.

Meanwhile, Wilks was setting a pattern. The 1933 underslung chassis car set a trend towards quality in the upper-medium price bracket that Rover would try to keep for more than sixty years. The car was the P1, but it was not called the P1 yet. The label was applied retrospectively as a sort of shorthand to distinguish the successive generations of Rover cars.

Wilks and Graham, together with Spencer's brother Maurice, now chief engineer, overhauled the organisation. Cars and components were built in too many places, so the old Meteor Works in Queen Victoria Road, Coventry, was sold and production concentrated at the Helen Street factory, renamed New Meteor Works.

Engines and transmissions were made at nearby Tyseley, and by the end of 1932 Rover was ready for recovery. By 1935-1936 matters had improved enough for Spencer Wilks to earn a commission in addition to his

salary of over £10,000, and the firm was building 6,000 cars a year. The Wilks era could begin in earnest.

The brothers' strategy was described by a reporter at the 1935 Motor Show: *'Stabilised design does not call for purely seasonal changes. During the last few years Rover cars have built up for themselves a reputation that excels the vast success of an old established company. They possess many characteristic features of construction and exhibit a distinct individuality in their road performance, whilst the coachwork continually gains prizes. Progress, however, has by no means been allowed to stand still. Rover designers are apt to invent or to adapt*

improvements rather earlier than most.'

The improvements could be seen and felt. Flexible engine mountings made Rovers quiet, the transmission freewheel made them easy to drive. The chassis was made thick and heavy where the stresses were greatest, thin and light where they were not. Graded frame stiffness, as it was called, made Rovers strong yet light and relatively cheap. The underslung rear suspension lowered the cars' centre of gravity, making them more stable and low-built. Wilks had an eye for style as well as engineering.

The P1 marked the arrival of Rovers with a strong sense of identity.

Winner of the 1907 TT Ernest Courtis poses with a road-going version of the winning car.
(left)

By 1939 Rover was building 11,000 cars a year and making profits of over £200,000. When the 1939-1945 conflict began, car production slowly ground to a halt. The last was made in May 1940. Rover was a member of the government's shadow factory scheme, which set up empty facilities for use in the event of war, and quickly began making aircraft engines at the rate of 80 a week.

It was the start of a five-year programme of war work which, besides Bristol Hercules and Armstrong-Siddeley Cheetah engines, included wings for Avro Lancasters, airframes for Albemarles, gas turbines and main components for tanks. The war saw Rover reaching into realms of technology of which pioneers such as Lewis and Clegg can scarcely have dreamt. It also precipitated the move to new premises at Solihull.

After the bombing of the Helen Street factory in 1940, Wilks rented part of his house at Street Ashton to the company, and in 1941 waived £10,000 of his £15,000 commission. He was "*...kind, courteous and considerate almost to a fault.*" Spencer Wilks's legal training clearly stood him in good stead during his stewardship because he "*... never lost his impressive calm in a crisis*".

Wilks ran Rover until he retired in 1962. Together with his brother Maurice he created Land Rover. At a

A redesign in 1937, together with technical changes that outlasted the war, marked a settling down. The changes were carried out on the car that came to be known as the P2. It consolidated the niche that Betjeman saw for it, with the wood and leather interiors, understated style, quiet running and supple ride that made it the car for people of taste and discrimination.

Rover ultimately outlasted Humber, Wolseley, Lanchester and industry trailblazers like Riley and Singer. It challenged them for the custom of such of the middle class as survived the Depression, then the war, with their spending power more or less intact. It always made a few sports cars, by way of demonstrating that Rovers were good enough to go fast, but by and large it was not a make of car that appealed to the fast and loose.

Its charm lay in less ephemeral qualities: ride, refinement, reliability, security, good paintwork, comfort and above all good taste.

Maurice Wilks, Rover's chief engineer throughout the critical 1930s and 1950s, lamented that refinement was always heavy. A Rover buyer could display good taste, but need not look for exciting performance. He looked as though he was making a clever choice rather than a thrilling one. It was subtle marketing, and Spencer Wilks identified it early.

time of real hardship for the luxury car industry, Land Rover was the lifebelt through which the make survived.

Maurice Wilks was educated at Malvern College and worked with General Motors before throwing in his lot with Spencer at Hillman. He directed Rover's technical programme for the best part of 40 years, and precipitated its entry into the field of gas turbine engines almost by chance. His wife met Sir Frank Whittle, then engaged in developing the jet engine.

Whittle proved a difficult partner, but from Rover's point of view their attachment was nothing short of momentous. It engaged Rover engineers at the leading edge of technology, a position they were able to exploit well after their direct connections with gas turbines had run down.

The turbine engine's inception went back to 1928, when Flight cadet Whittle claimed in a thesis written for the RAF College that the only way high-speed, high-altitude flight could be attained was through jet propulsion. He took out his first patent in 1930 without any encouragement from either the Air Ministry or industry.

Inventors were often tempted by the gas turbine, but because of the fierce temperatures and pressures it created its manufacture was regarded as well-nigh impossible. Its attraction for

aircraft lay in the limitations of propellers for speeds above 450mph, fully 200mph faster than anything flying in 1928.

In 1936 Whittle formed Power Jets Ltd to work on the development of jet engines. He tried to interest Armstrong-Siddeley, but met with deep scepticism. Eventually BTH (British Thomson-Houston)

produced drawings to Whittle's design for a turbo jet engine, the Whittle Unit (WU)1. It made formidable demands on the available metallurgy. The heat and stresses in the combustion chambers were 25 times what existing materials could cope with, yet an engine was built and began running on April 12, 1937.

A Morris Ten starter engine speeded it to about 2,300rpm before Whittle

opened the main fuel valve. The first experimental engine accelerated out of control and threatened to blow the test house to pieces. Whittle persevered, and by December 1940 the Air Ministry, under pressure to produce fighter aircraft that could outperform the Germans, supplied money for an improved W.1X.

This was followed by a contract for a practical flight engine, the W.1, which first ran on April 12, 1941, and flew in the Gloster E28/39 aircraft from Cranwell on May 15 with 850lb of thrust at 16,500rpm. The engine weight was 623lb and the aircraft's maximum speed was about 338mph in level flight.

The demand for a production engine was urgent, and the Wilks connection led to some of the world's first aircraft jets being built by Rover. By late 1941 Rover, BTH and Power Jets were building versions of the W.2 Mark 4 and the W.2B. A second Gloster aircraft, with a production Rover W.2B, inadvertently exceeded maximum revs and attained an astonishing 466mph, probably the fastest speed of any aircraft up to that time. If the war effort had not been so pressing, a Rover engine might have gained the world's absolute speed record.

The difficulties with Whittle proved insurmountable. The Wilks brothers and Rover engineer Adrian Lombard, later Rolls-Royce aero engines'

Winged Viking head radiator mascot of 1929. (left)

Avon tyres, Wilmot-Breedon bumper, pass-light and horn, Rover character re-emerges in post-war 14hp. (right)

director of engineering, contributed a good deal more to the development of the engine than Whittle ever gave them credit for. But the brittle relationship destroyed any hope of Rover becoming a major player in the jet engine story.

The inventor blamed Rover for delays in making the production engine, and claimed the firm had reneged on its agreement not to redesign any components. Rover, for its part, asserted that Whittle was obstructive and promptly redesigned the W.2B into the W.2B/26 with straight-through instead of reversed combustion chambers.

Rover engineer Gordon Bashford remembered the occasion:
"*Before we could start work on productionising the Whittle engine, to maintain secrecy we were sworn to secrecy over a Bible. We were segregated in a private area, converted from the directors' dining room at Rover's Helen Street factory in Coventry. There was a guard on the entrance and only people connected with the project were allowed in.*"

He was unrepentant about the redesign carried out by Maurice Wilks and Adrian Lombard. "*I think that Frank Whittle was upset because he had not thought of it first.*"

Matters came to a head in November 1942, when S G Hooker of

Rolls-Royce persuaded Lord Hives, his managing director, to intervene. Rolls-Royce was plainly anguished at the impasse between Whittle and Rover, which threatened to keep British jet aircraft out of the war.

Its motives were beyond reproach. Rolls-Royce was as concerned as Rover about equipping the Royal Air Force with the best aircraft. Yet it was eager not to be left out of an area of development vital to its aero-engine interests.

Rolls-Royce was committed to the Merlin and piston engines. Its only working alternatives were some rather unpromising turbo fans and turbo props, with a 14-stage contra-rotating gas generator, made in the Derby experimental shops.

Hives wanted a share in the Power Jets work and set up a staff at Derby to build a reliable W.1. Rolls-Royce's relationship with Whittle was certainly better than Rover's, and when Hives and Hooker met Spencer Wilks for a war-time dinner at the Swan & Royal in Clitheroe, they had a receptive audience.

Jet engines were not in Rover's line, said Hives. Wilks agreed, and said he would be relieved to be rid of the whole business. Hives's response was: *"You give us this jet job and I'll give you our tank engine factory at Nottingham."*

Rural reflections of the steering wheel in the twin-cylinder air-cooled Rover Eight of 1922. (left)

Rover regalia featured the Viking ship seized on as a jocular play on the connection between *Vikings* and *rovers*. (below)

From January 1, 1943, Hooker became chief engineer at the former cotton mill at Barnoldswick near Clitheroe, planned for W.2B production, but henceforth Rolls-Royce's jet engine development centre. The pace of development quickened and jets were soon in service with the Royal Air Force. A Rolls-Royce B.23 engine flew on the F9/40 Meteor on June 12, 1943, and a batch of 100 engines was delivered as the Welland 1 and went into action against V-1 flying bombs in August 1944.

Some of the technology that made the jet engine possible was a result of Rolls-Royce initiatives. The improvements in the compressors, which form the front half of a jet engine, came about through Rolls-Royce's superchargers developed for the Schneider Trophy seaplane contests won outright in 1931.

Yet Rover's place in the development of one of the 20th century's most demanding technologies is secure. It seconded some of its best engineers to the Rolls-Royce endeavour at Barnoldswick and Waterloo Hill, including Gordon Bashford, who was involved in much post-war car development.

The immediate effect was that Rover began making tank engines and relinquished, for the time being, its connections with gas turbines. It would never again involve itself with

aircraft jet propulsion engines.

Following the war Rover was preoccupied with cars afresh. Rovers had again begun to epitomise the well-behaved middle-class British car to a new generation beyond that of Betjeman's subaltern. Rover's symbolism as a return to a civilised way of life was secure. It was a calm, well-ordered car with a freewheel, and a silky engine with overhead inlet valves, a feature it shared with contemporary Rolls-Royces. Customers noted the similarity with satisfaction, an example surely of great minds thinking alike, for the arrangement was almost Rolls-Royce's and Rover's alone.

When peace came, the distinctive nature of the cars said more about their owners than titles, labels, job descriptions or social status. Rover had become a brand name beyond price; a brand name moreover nurtured not by publicity - Noble and his stunts had long gone - but by the calibre of cars carefully made and designed for a clientele that valued understatement, discreet comfort, silence and safety. Speed and acceleration were less consequential than good solid worth.

The affinity with luxury cars was sustained by a Rover's agreeable proportions and exemplary refinement. They were not flamboyant. A Rover's well-dressed interior of polished wood and supple leather exemplified good judgement, taste and discernment. It was once again the car of the professional, the doctor, the solicitor and the bank manager at a time when Ford, Austin and Morris furnished cars for the volume market, at prices between a quarter and a third less than Rover's.

Rover tried making lots of cheap cars in the 1920s but it had not come easily, and the management wisely rejected the radical two-cylinder air-cooled Scarab in 1931. It had the voguish features of the Volkswagen and other Continental small cars, but in its determination to match its products to its customers Rover decided it was unsuitable. The dealers sealed the little car's fate by refusing to sell it at a price that presupposed a reduced profit.

A post-second-war study for a small luxury car went the same way, and the first Rover to bear a P designation officially was the P3, when the P stood for Postwar. This was the independently sprung version of the P2, introduced in 1948.

In the 1950s Rover nearly became middle-aged as well as middle-class. It displayed great vigour in its research into gas turbines but was over-optimistic in imagining the difficulties of production would be quickly overcome.

Rovers grew quieter and more reliable, with the demeanour of coachbuilt classics and an almost Teutonic obsession with making progress through small changes. Completely new Rovers were rare. There were new engines, new chassis frames and new body shells, but not all at the same time. It was company policy to have a constant process of evolution rather than fundamental shifts.

A McKinsey study of German competitiveness in the post-war world identified the procedure as '... *a low-risk small-step approach to increasing the product value from generation to generation instead of making high-risk quantum-leap improvements in product design*'.

It was a policy that did not wholly survive the management upheavals of the 1960s, and by the 1980s was largely unnecessary because the technology of production engineering advanced so profoundly. It saw Rover through the middle years of the century with its reputation being constantly enhanced.

Detail changes, such as seven bearing crankshafts, were brought in because the engine ran more smoothly and more reliably. Rover kept an oil-level indicator on the facia for fastidious owners long after others had abandoned it, and small tell-tale plastic prisms above the sidelights so that drivers could see at once when they had a bulb failure.

The guns had long fallen silent before Betjeman's subaltern encountered a radical Rover. The fine proportions of the P4, with its Cyclopean eye centre pass-lamp, was as innovative in its way as Peter Poppe's hopeful overhead camshaft design of the 1920s. The P4 soon became the favourite car of the cultured classes and as imaginative as any British production car ever. The quintessence passed on easily, through the generations of the 1960s, when Rovers were again as dignified as Clegg's Edwardians.

The P4 was followed by the P5, the 3 Litre, a new strain of car with a

Rover 200 Coupé Turbo.
(below)

Viking ship was centrepiece of the reinstated radiator grille for 1992.
(right)

modern structure of such strength and integrity that it remained in production from 1959 to 1973.

It began life with a six-cylinder engine and ended with the splendid aluminium V-8 3.5-litre negotiated from America by another notable managing director, William Martin-Hurst, in the 1960s.

The Rover 2000 of 1963, the P6, was an automotive landmark. It bristled with technical novelty and had a vital new ingredient ensuring Rover's survival as an independent manufacturer through to the 1990s. It appealed to keen drivers.

"Rover was like a favourite aunt," one commentator noted, *"who suddenly lifted her skirts and ran. And ran better and faster than anybody ever thought she could run."* The auntie Rovers gave way to a new species of car that

purveyed excellence to a degree that brought it the first Car of the Year title ever awarded.

The 2000 appealed to owners wanting a lively turn of speed and good handling. It appealed to hearts and minds reared with confidence in Rover quality, a legacy of the great days of Rover's place as the car of the proficient driver, the experienced motorist.

It was an appeal so strong and so enduring that when in May 1986 Sir Graham Day was appointed chief executive of what had been variously British Motor Holdings, British Leyland, BL Cars and BL Ltd, he was able to conclude: *"One of the first things I was determined to do was alter public perceptions to catch up with the reality of improved products, and reflect our belief in producing quality specialist cars. In the course of research to decide which of our marques came closest in image and reputation to this ideal, one name consistently topped the list, overseas as well as at home - Rover."*

Now the name was making the car and not the other way round. Instead of creating something in the image of its customers, Rover had to make a car to fulfil what its customers understood as the Rover image.

It had to devise a car that would again match the name and reputation that

Carriages fit for a queen. Her Majesty the Queen's 3.5-litre P5 and an 800 Coupé at Windsor. (left)

Meteor makes a splash (below)

One of Britain's fine cars. A P4 advertisement from the 1950s. (right)

had been nourished by years of indoctrination, reputation, prestige and authority.

The new Rover Group plc had a task similar to that of Spencer Wilks nearly sixty years before. It had to create new models to suit the buyers, who knew what a Rover was about, and it had to create them quickly.

It was of no avail this time turning to one inspired engineer like Lewis or Clegg or Poppe for a solution. Entire new factories - new industries even - had to be created for the 1980s generation of Rovers, and new partners for their manufacture were found among the best engineers in the Far East, namely Honda.

The groundwork for the relationship was put in place by Sir Michael Edwardes for the Triumph Acclaim of 1981, a licence-built Honda Ballade. The partnership developed to joint and co-operative models, which kept the Rover identity secure. The last sixty years would have gone for naught if all Rover was going to do was build badge-engineered Hondas.

The styling, the decor, the trim, the suspension and many of the engines and transmissions of 1980s and 1990s Rovers remained the responsibility of Rover. The classic characteristics were retained, principally the quietness and refinement. Even fast Rovers were forbidden to be noisy. Their style remained understated. They had to stay discreet. The customers who Betjeman or Spencer Wilks might have recognised were still much the same as they had ever been, demanding cars as much at home at the manse or in the executive car park as at the golf club.

Rovers were not inexpensive, and although cheaper than limousines of the nobility and gentry, they were the archetypal executive car long before anybody ever thought of the term.

The management changes of the 1960s, and the industrial upheavals and flawed reliability of the 1970s, were repudiated only with difficulty. The surprise was that, following the confusion and the problems of controlling quality in a changing world, Rover's reputation survived at all. It said much for the distinction of the cars that had gone before that the good name was upheld.

It was heartened by the memories of Rovers past, as well as the surviving cars, in the hands of drivers who still felt they represented something less transient than passing fads and fashions.

Recreating Rover's reputation in the 1980s was a feat of some magnitude. Matching the car to the middle executive, who had taken on the moral mantle of the old middle class, was a triumph of good design. Stylishness

One of Britain's Fine Cars

THE ROVER COMPANY LIMITED · SOLIHULL, BIRMINGHAM also DEVONSHIRE HOUSE · LONDON

HOLLY LEAVES, 1953—37

could not to be bought at the expense of good taste; decorum could not be sacrificed for speed. Rover's traditionally conservative customers had to be carried along somehow with the new circumstances.

Insularity had no place in the new Rover. With so many Japanese ingredients the old isolationism was dead in any case. It was up to yet another new generation of management to achieve an

international flavour using distinctive British features.

It was not simply a case of using wood and leather for the interiors, although they were important; the qualities the customers expected had to radiate from the engineering of the cars. Rovers had to be Rovers in word, thought and deed.

Rovers had still to be exported and here some accidents of history were on the firm's side. Some traditional firms such as Burberry, or traditional products like single malt Scotch whisky, also found that their time had come.

British products that had survived the dark days of the 1960s were finding success in the rest of Europe, in particular France and Germany. Perversely, they were also finding success in Japan.

The years of doubt and confusion under the interim regime of the 1960s and 1970s were successfully set aside, and a second Rover revival, no less momentous than the first achieved under the Wilks regime of the 1930s, was ready to begin.

CHAPTER II

The Edwardians

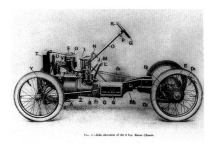

Rover primitive:
improved 8hp with
backbone chassis.
(above)

Rover's arrival into the world coincided with traffic becoming a social question. The Highways & Locomotives Acts of 1865 and 1878 repressed cars. Local councils imposed unrealistic conditions, including 2mph speed limits, and although the later act repealed the requirement for his red flag, an attendant walking ahead on foot was still required.

Matters slowly improved as the Locomotives on the Highways Act of 1896 gradually took effect. In 1903 the Motor Car Act authorised a speed of 20mph. Cars and motor buses proliferated to such an extent that the Board of Trade appointed a Royal Commission to examine congestion in London.

It reported on improvements in public transport. Extensions to the tube, new tram lines and a network of roads leading from the centre to the suburbs were proposed. The commission searched for ways of coping with the jams as horses gave way to motor cars. Unperturbed, Rover preceded the launch of its first petrol engine with

details of how its carburettor was going to work. Edmund Lewis displayed such resource in mixing the fuel and air in the constant-vacuum carburettor he designed for Rover that he was recruited from Daimler to design the entire car.

He declared that: "*The principle of the new Rover carburettor to a certain extent is normal, in that not only is the additional air admission regulated, but that (air) passing the jet is also regulated in volume and velocity.*"

A journalist was invited to try one and noticed the difference at once: "*Driving from Coventry to London I found there was an improvement of quite 20% in the power of my engine. I romped up hills.*"

It was a momentous time. In June 1903 a new era in motoring began with the formal incorporation of the Ford Motor Company in the United States, Henry Ford subscribing a quarter of the shares. In May 1904 the Honourable C S Rolls and Mr Henry Royce announced the partnership that created The Best Car in the World.

Rover primitive. A 1906
example of the 6hp pioneer
design of Edmund Lewis with
one cylinder of 780cc and
5.6 RAC horsepower.
(left)

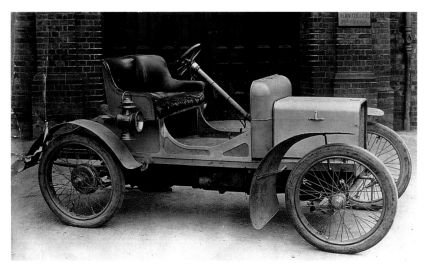

Both ends of the motoring spectrum came into being just as Rover announced its first car, pursuing a course somewhere in between. Rover knew its place in the scheme of things instinctively from the beginning. The quality car market was not yet defined as Edmund Lewis drew up an 8hp car that put a premium on good engineering, refinement and sturdy middle-class value.

He designed a light alloy backbone frame, a water-cooled engine and a three-speed sliding pinion gearbox. The single large water-cooled cylinder measured 114mm x 130mm and had a capacity of 1,327cc. It had Bosch ignition, side valves, was rated at 8.1 horsepower, and a prototype ran within six weeks. By the end of 1904 the chassis was on sale for £120. *Car Illustrated* thought the Rover Eight '*...set quite a new fashion*'. The

two-seater cost £200, a three-seater £220, and an export model with a stronger chassis and better ground clearance for "colonial" conditions (colonies were naturally assumed to have rough roads), £225.

Notwithstanding *Car Illustrated*'s enthusiasm, the Eight turned out less than a complete success. Lewis's radicalism proved its undoing. Bolting the rear axle firmly to the gearbox casing, and thence to the frame, was not a good idea, and the absence of rear springs gave a disagreeable ride. The backbone was terminated aft of the gearbox and a universal joint inserted into the drive line. The torque tube transmission thus created remained a feature of Rovers for much of the following three decades.

The gadget that employed engine compression to help out the brakes

was ingenious, but turned out complicated and expensive. The cam profiles were graded, and pressing a pedal altered the timing and duration of the valve openings. Closing the inlet valve, and making the exhaust valve open every revolution instead of every other, made every upstroke a compression stroke designed to create "*...a very powerful but absolutely smooth braking effect*".

Part of the backbone frame was even pressed into service to do duty as an 'exhaust box', and there were no rear springs. If there was no frame, ran Lewis's logic, and nothing to bolt springs on to, there was no need for conventional springs.

Instead the body was supported on long leaf springs at the back, and a transverse leaf spring at the front gave what Lewis called "three-point" suspension. This aimed to keep the mechanical parts of the car on the level while the body rolled and bobbed. It was introduced six years before the Model T Ford adopted something similar, and twenty years before the Austin Seven.

The Rover Eight remained in production until 1912, when it cost £265 10s for the two-seater, or £250 without hood and screen. It had high-sided doors and inside 'splashers'. It was carefully made and technically innovative, did a leisurely 900rpm but could be run up 'if desired', Rover

A 1904 8hp posed at the front door of the Meteor Works.
(left)

Workmen leave Meteor Works of the Rover Cycle Company soon after turn of the century.
(above right)

Rounded to fit on a bicycle's stem, the Rover shield.
(below right)

admitted rather diffidently, to 1,500rpm. Two enclosed flywheels weighed an imposing 120lb (about one-eighth the total weight of the car) to secure smooth running. In 1908 the gearchange was shifted to the right, but the curious camshaft brake which effectively turned the engine into an air compressor remained till the end. Wire-and-bobbin steering was not altogether satisfactory, but rack-and-pinion was available as a no-cost option.

By the close of the decade the Eight had a smart, open body with two comfortable, rounded seats. The tall windscreen was braced with leather straps fixed to the top of the frame, holding it upright against aerodynamic pressure at its top speed of about 24mph. High speeds might not inflict much strain on the straps, but it looked dashing, and the price was reduced to £200.

The Eight differed from other cars in two ways - it was well made and it was technically innovative. The light alloy backbone chassis looked strong, although the stiff springs set up stresses for which it turned out not strong enough. It was uncomfortable and it sustained breakages, and within months of its debut Lewis had to think again.

The bravura of the Eight gave way to a 6hp, which had a plain rectangular wood-and-steel chassis, and

straightforward half-elliptic springing. This time there were no technical *tours de force*. The engine was a thoroughly conventional, modestly dimensioned side valve of 780cc, with a single cylinder and water cooling by a gilled-tube radiator.

Lewis was loath to give up his attachment to substantial aluminium castings, and the crankcase with its outrigger engine mountings, clutch housing and gearbox were all in one piece. Unlike the Eight the entire car did not have to be split in two for servicing. The 6hp's castings were built with horizontal joints giving access to the interior. The aluminium casing reached almost to the back axle, with a short connecting shaft to the final drive. Reassuringly thick rods led to the external contracting rear brake shoes. Suspension was conventional by semi-elliptic leaf springs, and the

sprung back axle retained the Eight's torque-tube drive.

The occupants sat on, rather than in, a Rover Six overlooking the short stubby bonnet. The chassis members supporting the front springs, known as dumb-irons, projected ahead of the front wheels and a quadrant in front of the driver contained the ignition retard and advance. A novel ratchet arrangement on the pedal acted as a parking brake. The homely wooden body had shallow cutaway doors, and there were small dogcart steps instead of a full-length running board.

Rover's pursuit of a wide market with competitive prices did not permit frills, and luggage accommodation consisted of a box behind the seat with a hinged lid. The sole concession to style was a rakish tilt to the front mudguards. Some measure of refinement was attempted by attaching a light chain to the rear axle, preventing it twisting through torque reaction.

The upholstery had the style and comfort of a Victorian leather horsehair sofa, buttoned, hand-stitched and firm. There was little opportunity yet for Rover to display much elegance and fine finish, there were no instruments, and the woodwork was plainly varnished.

Lewis entered one of Britain's first motoring competitions on August Bank Holiday Monday, 1904, at Bexhill, where sprint meetings were held on the promenade.

Brooklands was still a wooded estate near Weybridge, and the first Grand Prix was years away, when 20,000 spectators crowded the sea-front roadway to watch Léon Serpollet's steam car swish silently along the kilometre straight at a dizzy 55mph. Outraged residents petitioned the Lord Chancellor's Court to prevent their peace and quiet being interfered with. Not all the 200 or so cars in Britain's first motoring competition were as quiet as M. Serpollet's, and the crowds that filled the hotels and upset the inhabitants seem to have been a noisy lot. The *Bexhill-on-Sea Observer* was none the less delighted: '*Bexhill has no objection to having its Arcadian quietness disturbed by millionaire motorists*,' adding perhaps a little cynically that '*the town reaped a harvest of golden grain*'.

Timing was by an elaborate electrical system laid out by Colonel Crompton, the founder of Crompton Parkinson, and although the objectors prevented a repetition of the event in 1903, it was run again in 1904.

'*One of the smallest cars making its debut and impressive on its first appearance was a new name in motoring, the Rover,*' according to the London magazine, *Car Illustrated*.

It was: '*remarkably free from vibration and gave a good account of itself, beating Mr Richard Lisle's Star in Class C, and a 10hp Ford in the semi-finals. It was only beaten by a more powerful Duryea. The name of the company producing the car is sufficient guarantee for the workmanship which has been put into it. Rover will be watched with interest because of its many points of peculiar novelty of design.*

'It seemed easy to manage, driven by the designer, the inspiration behind the first production Rover, Edmund W Lewis, formerly of Daimler.'

Sales of the Six after Bexhill were encouraging; twenty cars a week was good going. It remained in production alongside the original Eight for seven years, after Lewis left for a short-lived and unsatisfactory career with Siddeley-Deasy.

Lewis's outing at Bexhill convinced him of the value of motor sporting publicity. His last Rover, the 16/20 made from 1905 to 1910, won the 1907 Tourist Trophy race on the Isle of Man, and a production version of the TT car, the 20hp Tourer, established Rover as one of the leading manufacturers of the day.

The 16/20 was announced in July 1905 with four separately cast cylinders, the same size as the single (95mm bore and 110mm stroke) in Lewis's 6hp, making it a substantial 3,120cc. Like the Six it was later bored out to 97mm. Each cylinder could be removed separately from the crankcase and the crankshaft was machined from the solid.

The brake-assisting gadget survived, in a modified form, with a pedal that moved the cams backwards and forwards on a key-way on the camshaft. It was claimed to be a match for the car's normal friction brakes - not always much of a yardstick - and it

presaged modern variable-valve timing devices aimed at economy and improved exhaust emissions. Lewis was a bold innovator.

Lubrication remained a problem, and the 16/20 had an "irrigation" system in which oil thrown up by the flywheel was caught in a trough, which dripped it on to the big-ends through a series of 0.5in pipes. The engine once again constituted a load-bearing part of the framework back to the gearbox bell-housing, and the front transverse spring pivoted on a forward extension of the crankcase. The whole engine, suspension and gearbox could be unbolted and wheeled away for servicing.

The clutch displayed great ingenuity. It was an all-metal disc type, separate from the flywheel and *'contains no leather or fibre to burn or 'seize'',* according to Rover publicity of the time. The clutch shell had floating and fixed discs running in a bath of oil. When the pedal was operated the discs separated and the drive was taken up,

the oil being squeezed away so that moving off was gradual and smooth. *'Specially designed to prevent those jars and shocks which frequently occur to cars fitted with clutches of other character,'* according to Rover. *'As a matter of fact, the Rover Car never jumps away, but glides off from a standstill and picks up pace rapidly.'*

Rover was also deeply concerned about stopping. In addition to the engine brake, the 16/20 had drum brakes on the rear wheels and a transmission brake as well. *'The third brake, which, under all ordinary circumstances may not be called upon, and therefore may be termed an emergency brake, is applied by a side-lever actuating a band on a drum on the gearshaft.'*

Rover's affection for large aluminium castings persisted after Lewis's departure, and the 16/20's engine clutch and gearbox casings were bolted together in a unit.

'We claim, in thus encasing the whole of the working parts of the car, complete lubrication to all parts, as the casings themselves act as oil baths. No oil can exude, and, what is of equal importance, no dust, mud, or water can get at any vital portion of the machinery.

'In a similar way the differential gearing and back axle are provided with an aluminium covering,

Ernest Courtis celebrates his victory in the wet TT of 1907.
(left)

Rover managing director from 1902 to 1922 Harry Smith marked the occasion by presenting him with a watch.
(right)

thoroughly dust and waterproof, the differential case in itself being so constructed that lubrication for this portion of the transmission need not be renewed more frequently than once in a thousand miles.'

A thousand miles must have seemed a long way in 1905.

Standard bodywork was the *'highly popular 'Roi des Belges' type'*, with side-entrance. The upholstery *'...is of best'*, and colours were two shades of green, both called Rover Green, and one shade of red, called Rover Red.

For 50 years Rover was to be Rolls-Royce's middle-class shadow, and when Rolls-Royce won the Tourist Trophy Race on the Isle of Man in 1906, Rover cast an envious eye.

The race was organised by the Royal Automobile Club to test touring cars under road conditions, road closures for competition being forbidden on mainland Britain. The course was the one used for the 1904 Gordon Bennett races, with changes that cut out a northern loop to reduce disruption on the island. The first race was in 1905, and a Rolls-Royce finished second to a Scottish opposed-piston Arrol-Johnston. There was a good field of 44 cars.

Rover entered two cars, driven by Lewis and its chief test driver, Ernest Courtis, with satisfactory results.

Courtis finished fifth, half an hour behind the winning Arrol-Johnston, and Lewis was 12th.

In 1906 nine out of the 29 starters finished, the Hon Charles Rolls winning comfortably by 25 minutes, at an average of 39.3mph. The TT was not fast but, eager to promote competent touring cars, the organisers imposed a fuel consumption limit. It was fixed first at 22.5mpg, then stiffened to 25mpg.

In the 1907 race, run in a continuous drizzle round the shortened 40.5 mile circuit, Rover entered two 16/20hp models. Rolls-Royce entered as well but withdrew, partly because it believed the fuel consumption restriction irrelevant, partly because C S Rolls had become so enthused about flying that he was no longer interested. Rolls-Royce had made its point and would not take part in motor racing again.

Rover still had to make its mark. A heavy touring category, run concurrently with the main event, was for cars handicapped by an enormous vertical windscreen representing the height (8ft; 2.438m) of limousine body they were expected to carry.

They were also expected to average 16mpg, and of the 22 trophy cars in Rover's class, only two completed their set six laps (240.5miles; 387km). Courtis covered the course at 28.8mph

(46.35kph), 5mph slower than Percy Northey's Rolls-Royce in second place at 33.7mph (54.64kph) in 1905, and more than 10mph slower than Rolls in 1906. But he won the race by 12 minutes in taxing conditions.

Most of the failures were due to fuel shortage or ignition systems drowned by the drenching rain. Courtis's principal accomplishment was finishing ahead of the Beeston-Humber that won the heavy touring class.

The winning Rover had two useful assets. It was one of the lightest cars in the race, and the engine braking device helped it work against a target fuel consumption. Closing the inlet valve

One month from the date of ordering, a new owner could drive home in a 16/20. Price was £400 complete with hood, screens and bulb horn. (left)

Wood-rimmed wheel and ignition controls, 8hp. (right)

altogether on downhill stretches gave a useful improvement in economy, an example followed by a number of economy cars introduced during the fuel crises of the 1970s.

At the motor show in the autumn of 1907 Rover presented its 20hp Tourist Trophy production model with twin Stepney wheels, heart-shaped radiator and a catalogued top speed of 45mph. The elegant four-seat tourer's engine was bigger than the TT car's, and there was an extra 4in on the wheelbase.

The RAC rating was now 23.3hp and it was priced at £450. Yet despite its success neither it nor the 12hp four-cylinder models of 1908 and 1910 proved very successful.

Rover entered the TT again in 1914, winning the team prize over the island's rough roads and mountainous tracks, with Bush Newsome, A J Lindsay from Rossleigh, the

Edinburgh dealer, and Douglas Brown, son of the proprietor of the *Isle of Man Times*.

Rover's assault on the motorcycle market, with the 3.5hp single-cylinder side-valve 500cc Imperial, was brief, but not altogether unsuccessful.

After examining every machine in the Cycle and Motorcycle Show at Olympia in 1910, Dudley Noble concluded that the Rover appeared a close copy of the 3.5hp Triumph motorcycle: '*The main difference was that the Rover had a red cross on its tank instead of the Triumph's green panels. Right away I decided that Rover was going to have the privilege of my services even if the management did not yet know it.*' Noble worked as a temporary assistant at the show and was so impressed that he joined Rover as a motorcycle test rider.

Demand for the 3.5hp was healthy, despite a bothersome tendency for early examples to destroy their engines. Some of the cylinder castings proved to be porous near the exhaust valve, and a blowhole could develop with such explosive effect that the top of the combustion chamber parted company with the cylinder. This caused the compression tap to blow off and pierce the petrol tank with disastrous results.

The launch in 1909 of the 'Silent Knight' engined cars at Olympia

proved something of a disaster. Bernard Wright, who was in charge of engineering, persuaded the board to accept the sleeve-valve engines that Daimler was building under licence in Germany. For the next three years, this power unit dominated the range, even appearing on single-cylinder models.

The Knight engine had two cylindrical slide valves, with inlet and exhaust ports, moving between the cylinders and pistons. The engines were offered at a premium of £30. Patrons were expected to pay extra for the smoothness and quietness that would become a Rover custom. The advantages claimed included long periods of 25,000 to 30,000 miles before decarbonising, an important consideration when many engines needed overhauls at less than 10,000 miles.

The tally of 2,500 purchasers of Daimler engines was imposing. They were scrupulously advertised in order of precedence, beginning with His Majesty the King, Her Majesty the Queen, His Imperial Majesty the Czar, Her Imperial Majesty the Empress Dowager of Russia, and His Majesty the King of Spain, down through royal dukes of Sparta, Battenburg and Connaught, by way of humbler crown princesses to the most servile nobility and gentry. Yet despite such a distinguished clientele, the engines were persistently smoky and mostly

Motorcycle manufacture continued until well after the war (below), long after the elegance of the 20hp tourer, based on the TT winner, was an Edwardian memory. (right)

The 350 c.c. ROVER Motor Cycle for 1925

 **ROVER**

(Above). A front view of the 12 h.p. Overseas Model Rover Car, showing the sturdy front axle and steering details. No part of the chassis is within 10 ins. of the ground.

(Below). The side curtains can be left in situ with the hood lowered, thus protecting the passengers at both front and rear of the car from side draughts. Note the spring panel in the side curtains to permit of the driver signalling. The side curtains open with the doors.

unable to cover the large mileages claimed without overhaul.

The next charismatic engineer to influence the development of Rover was Owen Clegg. Born in Leeds in 1877, he trained, like so many engineers of his generation, in railway workshops. He joined Wolseley in 1904, but was induced by Vickers to run a company in Glasgow before joining Rover in 1910. With Clegg as works manager, Rover production increased from 400 cars in 1911 to 1300 in 1912, and was still expanding when he left on the eve of the war to take over the Darracq factory in Paris.

Wolseley was a significant manufacturer, so Clegg was something of a catch, and brought not only Wolseley expertise but also a number of his design colleagues. He set to work at once on a car that aimed to cast aside the smoky failures of the Knight sleeve valves. He introduced a poppet-valve 12hp car in 1912 that was solid, dependable and strong. It became famous as the Clegg Twelve, and remained Rover's standard model until the middle of the 1920s. It had four cylinders cast in a block, of 75mm bore and 130mm stroke, giving a capacity of 2,298cc. The inlet ports were cast in the head, it had a water-jacketed carburettor, worm drive to the back axle and electric lighting. Rovers were still made at the first Meteor works on the constricted site in the centre of Coventry, stretching from behind the showroom at Hertford Street to Queen Victoria Road. The coachworks were half a mile or so away in Cheylesmore, and to ease production bottlenecks Rover adopted a policy similar to Henry Ford's famous any-colour-so-long-as-it's-black.

By painting the cars a standard pastel green, unless the customers specified otherwise, the finishing processes were speeded up and the cars gained a distinctive appearance. Rover continued to use the colour on many of its cars up until 1939.

Clegg's Rovers looked robust and well proportioned, and among their technical assets was efficient lubrication. The oil baths of previous years were never up to the job, and this time the designer was careful to include a proper oil pump.

The improvements Clegg made to production methods were lasting. By 1912 Rover had its own foundry, and Clegg imposed disciplined techniques including batch construction, with groups of cars assembled almost on mass-production lines.

The Rover Twelve sold well, and the batch system increased the number of a single model made in the modest factory from a few dozen to several hundred a year.

The Twelve was available as a rakish two-seater with Lucas starting and lighting set, hood, screen, spare wheel and tyre, for £700. It was also obtainable as a two-seater chassis for only £600 and a limousine coupé with an upright closed body at £800. By 1914 it was the only Rover in production, often with tall, taxi-like saloon bodywork and rear doors, landau hood-irons, spare wheel and roof rack. It had the characteristic Rover radiator, a top speed of 45mph, and cost £475.

The price included items normally regarded as extras, such as the windscreen, hood, paraffin side and tail lamps, a spare wheel and a bulb horn. Electric lighting, and what were still known as 'self-starters', were rare, and headlamps such as Lucas 'Kings of the Road' were usually bought separately.

Rover asserted that the car reintroduced at the end of the war was changed only in detail, but the alterations were significant. The engine dimensions remained the same, but it now had a detachable cylinder head with a separate exhaust manifold, instead of one cast within the cylinder block. The new head improved breathing and the power was increased by around 50 per cent. Its RAC rating of 13.9hp earned it the title of Rover Fourteen, and it now had handsome electric headlights attached to the radiator shell.

The induction side of the Fourteen engine was still formed within the block, but the flow to the valves was easier, and there was more space for cooling water.

Clegg improved the lubrication system before he left, and oil was now driven under pressure through a gallery in the crankcase. The camshaft was chain

driven and another chain drove the magneto on the offside.

Rover detailing was constantly improving. The pistons of the Fourteen had four rows of holes drilled in the waist and skirt, and an

extra ring went through the centre of the gudgeon pin to prevent it from rotating. Lighter pistons meant less reciprocating weight, better response and smoother running. There were few changes to the chassis; suspension was by semi-elliptic springs. The two-

The painted wheels of the 20hp (right) gave way to the practicality of the Clegg Twelve.
(left)

seater now cost £525, and the most expensive model was the limousine coupé, at £750. The gearbox was smaller and the underslung worm drive was retained.

The Fourteen had what *The Autocar* called '*a greatly improved silhouette*', achieved mostly by taking the petrol tank from the dash, where it fed the carburettor by gravity, to the back, where it had a vacuum feed.

Yet despite the success of the Fourteen Rover was uncertain of how to progress following the increase in business during the war. Turnover was up from £320,000 in 1911 to over £1 million in 1920. Rover finished the war with a good deal of extra capacity, and some of the directors were convinced the company was now big enough to tackle the volume market.

But there was disagreement on what sort of cars it ought to make. On the one hand, there seemed plenty of wealthy industrialists flush with cash earned in war time, who were likely to spend it on large, expensive cars. Their numbers might be small but the returns from costly cars were good. It was still only the well-to-do who could afford cars at all, and there seemed little future at the cheap end of the market.

On the other hand, large numbers of small economical cars might meet the requirements of a generation that had

come through the war at a car-buying age and was now in a car-buying frame of mind. The euphoria of returning to peace-time production encouraged Rover to conclude that at last it could match Austin and Morris in numbers.

The demobilised generation was, alas, impoverished, and not many of the returning heroes could afford cars. Despite this, transportation became a post-war obsession, and one of the curiosities it came up with was the cyclecar. This was something between a motorcycle and a car, and tended to be spindly and air-cooled.

Cyclecars were heavier than motorcycles and less powerful than cars, lacking speed, comfort and often much in the way of weather protection. Some had a certain rakish style; most tended to be less than stable. Rover took the view that although the market might want something simple, it could manage something better.

Rover also needed something besides the robust Clegg Twelve/Fourteen if the spell of austerity looked like being prolonged. If there were not enough post-war riches to go round, the returning survivors deserved an economical small car to brighten up the 1920s.

Rover acquired the design for a new 8hp, together with a prototype and the former Component Munitions factory

at Tyseley, from Jack Sangster, a Birmingham entrepreneur fresh out of the army. Before the war Sangster's father had been involved with Ariel motorcycles and the Swift light car, and the factory (which made fuses) was looking for an occupant.

The deal with Rover included Jack Sangster's appointment as assistant works manager, a substantial investment of £400,000 raised by extra share capital, and an agreement that the new car would be assembled at Tyseley and taken to Coventry to have its bodywork put on. When it went into production, the Eight had a 998cc twin-cylinder air-cooled, side-valve engine, whose cylinder dimensions coincided with those of Rover's 3.5hp motorcycle. It was, in effect, two of the 500cc motorcycle cylinders laid flat, with a roller-bearing crankshaft in the middle, and gave 14bhp.

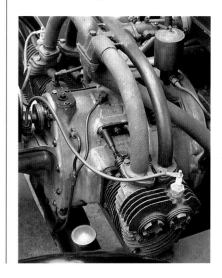

The tiny twin cylinder engine of the Rover Eight. Finned cylinder heads stuck out into the airflow; inlet and exhaust pipes curved over the top. (right)

Generous air intake for the Rover Eight (above) offered with daintily proportioned two-seater body (right). This was Britain's best economy car until the water-cooled Austin Seven.

Lubrication was by an oil pump which drew from a separate tank underneath the engine and delivered through adjustable drip feeds into the top of the crankcase.

It was not fast, managing 30-35mph at a modest 1,800rpm, and although the three-speed gearbox had wide-spaced ratios to enable it to climb hills, the engine was somewhat asthmatic. But there was little opposition. The Model T Ford had the wrong cylinder dimensions for the British market, so it was heavily taxed, and there was something of a gap between the simple cyclecars and the typically large and heavy tourer.

The Eight's simple channel section frame had quarter-elliptic springs at each end, and the car was equipped with a disc clutch, worm final drive and rack-and-pinion steering. There was electric lighting but no electric starter until one was offered as an option in 1923.

A total of 17,000 Rover Eights, with their distinctive disc wheels and puffing air-cooled twins, were sold up till production ended in 1924. It was a substantial number in an era when annual production generally totalled hundreds rather than thousands, and tens or hundreds of thousands were only realised in America.

The wheelbase of the Eights was extended to 7ft 10in and the engine increased to 85mm bore x 100mm stroke, giving a capacity of 1,134cc.

The Eight revived a name that had been a cornerstone of Rover's early reputation, and together with the Fourteen it made a good range. But the chassis was crude even for a car so cheap, and the appearance painfully plain.

The cylinders stuck out from the sides into the airstream to help cooling, but were the source of sporadic difficulties for the hard-working little twin. Although quite well balanced and smooth, the engine was inclined to cast off its cylinder heads at high revs. Heat distortion seems to have been the cause of the affliction and it was never completely cured. The sluggish acceleration was also difficult to ignore. The Tapley gradient meter cheerfully offered as an extra was never going to register much in the way of pull.

The weight was 10cwt, the Treasury rating 8.8hp, and the complete car cost £220. Special paintwork was £5, side curtains to a hood completely enclosing the body £3, and a flush-fitting speedometer was £7.

Despite its artless demeanour, the Eight had a flattering welcome and one magazine said: '*It seems likely to uphold Rover's familiar reputation for reliability and good service. When a little cheap car is evolved by a first-rate firm many people are naturally greatly interested.*'

The Eight turned out to be engaging if only because of its exasperating eccentricities. Several were adapted for racing at Brooklands with bullet-shaped bodies and exposed wheels. The glowing cylinder heads and the crude detailing could be forgiven only up until the advent of the Austin Seven. Its seemingly unburstable water-cooled, four-cylinder engine and upright stance made the Eight seem merely uncouth.

In some desperation Rover offered the Eight as a practical looking commercial traveller's car at £160, with a two-seat body and a large box on the back.

Dudley Noble, by now Rover's publicity manager, did not have an easy time promoting the little car. Air-cooling in particular was suspect, and to provide reassurance on this and other aspects of reliability he arranged a drive from Land's End to John o'Groats without stopping the engine. It took place under RAC scrutiny, and would have been a success had a driver not stalled the engine in Bristol traffic.

The reality was that by 1923 the Rover Eight was already in decline. Rover was not the only manufacturer to spot the gap in the market; Herbert Austin had been thinking along the same lines, and the four-seater the size of a motorcycle and sidecar he drew up in

his Bromsgrove billiard room revolutionised car design much as the Mini did 40 years later.

Austin's approach to a small car was to miniaturise a big one, unlike Rover, whose Eight was in some respects little better than an enlarged cyclecar. Both approaches were logical enough, but Austin's proved the more enduring.

The keynote of the Austin Seven was simplicity, and despite a derisive reception by the press when it was announced in 1922, it was a resounding success. The Baby Austin defeated the cyclecar with the features of full-sized cars although its performance was modest, acceleration leisurely and luxuries such as an electric starter, coil ignition and four-speed gearbox were postponed to later versions. It had four wheel brakes - the pedal worked the rear ones and the handbrake those at the front -and a contemporary road test complained that it took 56 feet to accomplish a stop from 30mph.

It hardly seemed to matter. The Seven's modest performance was easily controlled. So far as Rover was concerned it was a formidable competitor, it looked like a full-sized car, and even behaved like one. Exports flourished. The Austin Seven was built in France as the Rosengart, in the United States as the Bantam, and was even copied illegally by Datsun in Japan. It was launched in Germany by Dixi and reached the market in 1927 as

the first-ever BMW. It completely overwhelmed Rover's alternative. But for it the Eight might have been more of a success. There was no disgrace in being eclipsed only by a car that lasted, in one form or another, from the end of the first world war right up to the beginning of the second.

Yet if the air-cooled Eight was rough and ready, the four-cylinder, water-cooled 1,074cc 9/20 designed to replace it was staid and undistinguished. Contrived in some haste, the Nine sold for £215. Front-wheel brakes were added in 1926, and in 1927 it was offered with a detachable hard-top.

There was an air of desperation about Noble's stunts to help promote it. He arranged for the RAC to choose one off a showroom floor and see how far it could be driven for £5. Two girls were put behind the wheel for the sake of the publicity, and it did 2,147 miles on petrol at 1s 8½d (8.5p) a gallon and oil at 5s 8d (28.3p). The cost of replacing damaged or broken parts had to be included, but the labour charge for replacements was assumed to be covered by the guarantee.

The Honourable Victor Bruce, who won the 1926 Monte Carlo Rally, complained that managing 2,000 miles on £5 was only a result of the British 20mph speed limit, and challenged Rover to do the same on the Continent. Noble obliged with another exploit in 1924, in which an

Country house elegance of the Rover 12hp. (left) This 1912 car was for many years in the Sword collection in Scotland until re-acquired by the company.

Sturdy Viking acquired a battleaxe in 1922. (below)

open four-seater 9/20 managed a 30mph average in France and much the same fuel consumption. The run was again carried out under RAC observation and Noble's reward was an enhanced advertising budget for the following year.

Rover was still hedging its bets. The Eight was replaced by the 9/20 with the same chassis and a four-cylinder engine. Just in case demand for a larger car materialised, it also recklessly revised its programme in 1923 to include a 21hp 3.5-litre Six with side valves. Departing for once from its attachment to integral construction of the power train, the engine was directly mounted in the chassis, with the gearbox carried separately on a cross-member. It had the shortest production run of any Rover and only three were ever built.

Engineers came and went but none quite managed to replace the energetic Owen Clegg. Rover was in need of a new designer, and Dudley Noble was called in to discuss who should be appointed to get on with the job of replacing the Fourteen. Jack Starley, son of the founder, J K Starley, told him that Rover had £150,000 cash in the bank, and the new car had to "*appeal to the middle-class buyer who appreciated quality and wanted reliability*".

Starley had the right idea, but the result was a disaster that nearly

bankrupt Rover, and discredited him as managing director.

There were two finalists for the job, Major H E Barker of HE, a sports car manufacturer, and Peter August Poppe, a Norwegian. Poppe had the advantage. He already had a design in his pocket for a four-cylinder engine with hemispherical combustion chambers, an overhead camshaft, and 45-degree inclined valves. It looked like the specification either of a racing car, or a sophisticated middle-class tourer of the first rank. Poppe's car had a four-speed gearbox and a spiral bevel back axle, and seemed to be exactly what Starley was looking for.

He was an engineer with the best credentials, for Poppe was not only experienced, he had a reassuring reputation in the industry. Born in 1870, he founded the engine firm of White and Poppe in 1899, with Alfred White, son of a director of Swift's, the big Coventry bicycle makers. White's family provided the money, and Poppe's engineering skills, developed at Steyr in Austria, supplied the technical wisdom.

Yet Poppe's greatest asset, to a manufacturer still toying with the idea of competing with industry giants such as Austin and Morris, were his connections. It was he who influenced William Morris to establish his business on the basis of bought-in engines, components, gearboxes and

axles. As suppliers of engines for Morris, White and Poppe became one of the largest producers in Britain.

It enjoyed a reputation for precision and developed industry-wide standards for components. Interchangeable parts reduced costs and improved quality and serviceability, and Peter Poppe had been instrumental in introducing them.

White and Poppe made money in armaments, and by the end of the war bought its factory. White wanted to sell out, but Poppe wanted to move into car manufacturing. White's financial clout won the day and the firm was sold to Dennis Brothers. Poppe stayed on for two years before looking elsewhere, first as a consultant at Maudslay, then to seek a job with Rover.

A director of Rover and Maudslay, Alec Craig, encouraged the Rover board to engage Poppe, and set him to work on the car he had in mind. It was to be called the 14/45.

Despite its shortcomings the 14/45 was a turning point for Rover. Poppe was strong minded and radical, which he demonstrated in the cylinder head design of one of the first production cars to have inclined valves, hemispherical combustion chambers and a central sparking plug. It was a layout endorsed by theoreticians for its efficiency and good breathing, the combustion chamber shape was ideal,

Poppe's elegant engine in the 16/50; four cylinders 2.5-litres, overhead camshaft, made largely of aluminium yet the car was too heavy and costly. (left)

and Poppe was given the funds to develop it.

The valves were operated by an overhead camshaft driven from the back of the crankshaft. The inlet valves operated directly through rockers, and the exhaust valves on the other side had horizontal tappet rods passing between the cylinder heads. The problematical area was lubrication, and although the camshaft and tappets were submerged in an oil bath, the engine tended to leak.

The lubrication system demanded careful production. It was the first Rover with oil fed under pressure to the big-ends. Oil was pumped up into the valvegear, round the engine, and then still under pressure went to the gearbox and steering. The steering box was firmly mounted on the engine to help damp out vibrations.

Poppe was not universally liked at Rover. Noble for one distrusted him, complaining that his English was poor and his slide-rule was used mainly for effect. Noble disliked Poppe's habit, when faced with difficult questions, of lighting a large pipe to gain thinking time. He complained Poppe let the match burn his fingers to get off without replying at all.

The works director, Mark Wilde, resigned on the spot when he saw the complexity of the cylinder head. Poppe claimed that the 14/45 would weigh

EXTREME accessibility is the keynote of the engine design, and any owner can remove cylinders or cylinder heads, adjust the magneto, and inspect the oiling system, etc., easily and quickly. The engine being set in the chassis in an inclined position puts the starting handle at the best height from the floor to ensure ease of operation without stooping, and keeps the transmission as nearly as possible in a straight line right to the back axle, so obviating friction and wear on the universal joints. The simple method of changing a wheel by removing three nuts only will be noticed.

25cwt, do 25mpg and 65mph and sell in open four-seater form for £450. The car turned out to be overweight, the fuel consumption was heavier than predicted, and it was wide of the estimated price by £100. It only managed 60mph and the camshaft drive was noisy and troublesome. It attracted a good deal of attention at the 1924 Olympia motor show - an overhead camshaft was still rare - but the businesslike and practical 14hp Hillman, designed rather like Major Barker's HE, might have been more circumspect.

Insufficiently powerful to carry the heavy limousine bodies that were in vogue, the 14/45 was replaced in May 1925 by the 16/50, with the engine enlarged to 2,413cc by increasing the bore of the cylinders. The noisy drive gears remained an affliction and it was still stubbornly underpowered. It won the RAC Dewar Trophy for 50 consecutive ascents of Bwlch-y-Groes, the stiff 1.5 mile Welsh hill, but it was the downfall of Jack Starley. He was sent off to visit a Rover dealer in Melbourne, Australia, received compensation of £4,500 and resigned.

The 16/50 was well received at the time, and critics enthused about the smooth running of the engine, vigorously prompted by Noble's publicity: '*It has the smoothness of running usually associated only with a six cylinder engine, yet with this silky pull there is combined the superior efficiency of four cylinders. Indeed, many experienced motorists prefer the 16/50hp Rover engine to the majority of Sixes because there is such a pleasing absence of 'fussiness', and, of course, the working parts of the engine are less numerous.*'

Owen John, esteemed by Rover as one of the leading motoring critics, wrote fulsomely and at length in *The Autocar*: '*What exactly does a driver - and in these days most drivers are owner drivers - want in a car? He wants first and foremost, an engine that will do exactly what he wants it to do, and go, fast or slow, where he wishes it to go and he gets it here to perfection, together with economy of fuel, comfort in driving, and a nippiness in steering that has to be experienced to be believed.'*

It stretches the imagination to think of the cumbersome 16/50 as 'nippy', although as the catalogue said: '*Owen John's good opinion is shared by many another experienced motorist, for there is undoubtedly a 'something' about this fine production of one of the most reputable concerns in the British motor industry that stamps it with a seal of high distinction.'*

The catalogue continued: '*The now famous 16/50 hp Rover has the combination of six-cylinder smoothness of running with the greater efficiency and lower operating costs of the medium-powered four-cylindered car. Until you looked beneath the bonnet, you would imagine that there must be six instead of four silent cylinders to provide such a flow of silken power, and the car sweeps along with such remarkable lack of effort and hurry that the speedometer can scarcely be believed, until a combination of milestones and clock completely vindicate the instrument. That is, perhaps, one of the chief charms of the advanced design - the ability to maintain a high average speed without any sensation of 'forcing' the car.'*

The catalogue was specific about the advantages of the hemispherical combustion chambers. The advantages of the spark plug being in the middle made detonation less likely. The

description of the engine emphasises the advantages of the single camshaft. Two would duplicate friction and the tappet rods '*...run horizontally across the head perpetually lubricated by an entirely automatic supply of oil forced there by the pump which feeds every bearing in the engine under pressure*'.

It also enthused over the engine's construction: '*It is well known that to attempt to reduce weight by lightening these parts is a primary cause of vibration and harsh running, and it must be borne in mind that when an engine sets up vibration, power which should be delivered at the road wheels is being dissipated in the process: hence the axiom that vibration is a thief of power.'* The catalogue writer could have been drawing up a Rover catechism for subsequent engineering achievements.

Rover consistency shone through in the supply of lubricant to the transmission. '*Gearbox, steering gear and clutch receive their supply of lubricant from the three gallons of oil carried in the engine sump whence it is distributed throughout the entire unit by a mechanical pump.'*

The large capacity of the sump was regarded as a virtue, because it ensured that the oil remained clean and cool, reducing the frequency with which the owner must inspect the level. '*It is possible to run for long distances without having to replenish the sump*

(so long, of course, as the pressure indicator on the facia board records the circulation of the oil).'

The four-wheel brakes of the 16/50 seemed to answer the 1920s motorist's dread of skidding. The danger was all due, according to Rover, to unequal braking pressure, '*...even with the usual type of compensating gear*'. By equalising the braking pressure to each wheel a Rover could be stopped rapidly '*...on any surface without there being the least sensation of skidding*'. Poppe's son Olaf became works manager at Rover, but Colonel Searle sacked Poppe Snr in 1930 on payment of £2,000 compensation and threatened Olaf with six months' notice to quit.

The handsome 16/50 Doctor's Coupé of 1927 illustrated the direction Rover was taking. It reflected the market Rover would make its own, and even though it was one of the heaviest Rovers ever, it carried the reassurance of a car built to last. It was designed to appeal to reputable members of the community, professional opinion-formers, in this case doctors.

It was a car with doors that closed with the convincing clunk of a railway carriage, interiors trimmed with wood and leather, and an instrument panel with clear clock-faces. It had furnishings that looked like those in a doctor's sitting room or even a consulting room, door cappings with fine inlays, and door pockets with

Cigar-smoking customer with spats seems a bit up-market for a modest Rover Eight. Two-spoke steering wheel was not the only novel feature. (left)

leather flaps like giant tobacco pouches. The Doctor's Coupé was a car for strong men in plus-four tweed who preferred things built to last.

The bonnet was not over-long. Large engines were pretentious and a four-cylinder did not need a lot of space, yet the view over it was imposing. Dignified Lucas headlamps sprouted from the radiator cowl and the sidelamps were huge, round globes on the wings - everything about the car was proportioned generously. The engine had smart polished aluminium valvegear covers, exquisitely finished on the outside to promote the belief that it was just as carefully done on the inside. The tiny Zenith carburettor looked small for the

job and a spare set of spark plugs was screwed to the bulkhead.

The running board carried a polished wood box for the accumulators and a toolbox with a suitcase-style locking catch, and there was a huge filler cap for the vulnerable-looking petrol tank underneath the passenger. The running boards had foot scrapers and many owners proudly displayed a warning triangle at the rear saying 'Four Wheel Brakes' - technology already had snob appeal. The RAC rating was 15.9hp, top speed 55mph and the price £675.

Poppe tried to counter the car's reputation for being overweight by building a single-seater version, with two Stromberg carburettors, 7:1 compression and bigger valves.

A tall car with a large Rover radiator, it lapped the Brooklands track driven by Erling Poppe at over 100mph. A two-seater sports 16/50 gained an RAC certificate at Brooklands at a speed of 83.94mph.

The huge 16/50 proved to be the end of an era. Not many were made, and all that remained when Spencer Wilks took over was the whiff of quality and an aura of respectability.

Six-cylinder engines were becoming fashionable. It was surprising how well Rover's reputation survived the 16/50's high price, ponderous performance and erect appearance.

When the Rover Ten edged its way in, with chrome-plated brightwork and optional sunshine roof for the 1928 season, it was accepted as a proper Rover. It had the engine of the old 9/20, with an extra 3mm on the cylinder bore, making a capacity of 1,185cc.

The Ten Special was brought in by the newly appointed Wilks, with a body that owed a good deal to a Hillman Minx.

The supplier who made the steel pressings for both companies was not above a certain commercial opportunism. Rover needed a new car urgently, Wilks's father-in-law was William Hillman, and there was little attempt to disguise the similarity.

The resemblance hardly mattered, nobody seemed to notice it, and the Special did 3,800rpm with a steady 27bhp against the basic model's 3,600rpm and 25bhp.

There was pump cooling for the Special, pump and fan for the basic, and both cars had pushrod overhead valves and a two-bearing crankshaft. A three-speed gearbox was standard, four-speed optional, and top speed was 57mph. The Ten kept much the same Hillman-based body with no enclosed luggage boot and an external spare wheel until 1937.

Rovers with special coachwork tended

to have names with colonial connections such as Nizam, the semi-sports two-seater made by Carbodies; Rajah, a semi-sports four-seater by Whittaker and Mitchel of London; Ranee, a foursome drophead coupé made by George Maddocks of Huntingdon; and Maharajah, a four-door semi-sports saloon made by Weymann at Addlestone.

Now Rover began displaying its proudly middle-class pedigree. As it headed for renaissance, it used a new advertising slogan 'One of Britain's Fine Cars'. With its new-found self-confidence there came another car that was to be a landmark in its history; Rover launched its first six-cylinder.

Substantial radiator (left) of the 1927 16/50, the celebrated Doctor's Coupé (right), which showed Rover dedicated to large aluminium castings and deep oil baths twenty years after Edmund Lewis. Price new £675.

CHAPTER III

Drive towards Hastings

By 1928 Rover's losses had started to come under control, and following the appointment Sir Alfred Mays-Smith to the board and Frank Ward as general manager, they had been reduced to £78,000. They were hard years. Of the 36 British manufacturers at the Olympia motor show, only six were declaring a dividend to shareholders.

Rover shareholders demanded more action, and Herman Jennings from Sheffield and W D Sudbury from Matlock joined the board and demanded the retirement of Colonel W F Wyley, who had been Rover's chairman since 1909.

Wyley left disillusioned, and in his place they installed Mays-Smith's nominee, Colonel Frank Searle, to appoint new leaders in management and engineering. Searle quickly set about reducing the workforce, dispatched J K Starley on his world tour, and began to plan a new car. Peter Poppe was instructed to set a new course, draw up a modest medium-sized saloon, and equip it with a six-cylinder engine.

There were no fancy overhead camshafts for Rover's first six. This time Poppe designed a forthright 65mm x 101.6mm, 2,023cc pushrod unit for a plain family car of high quality and modest performance. All that remained of its predecessor was the Weymann body, and the new model became known as the Light Six 16hp, selling for £325. There was a coachbuilt saloon for £345, or at £385 a Sportsman's Saloon with hide upholstery, folding roof and luggage boot.

The Weymann fabric body was not a success. It deteriorated quickly and many customers were disillusioned. It was sometimes held to blame for the company's troubles, but they were more deep-seated than that.

Poppe designed a clean-looking and well-finished engine, with the cylinders cast integrally with the upper part of the crankcase, and a four-bearing crankshaft. He paid careful attention to the shape of the combustion chamber, and the upper end of the cylinder barrel was enlarged to form the combustion space. The

Most Meteors emerged from the factory with rather staid bodywork. This upright saloon had bumper and radiator Viking ship badges, but no helmeted warrior on the prow.
(above)

One of two cars with sedance bodywork by Corsica, British Motor Heritage's Meteor had 3 SU carburettors, and was exported to South Africa after completion in April 1930.
(left)

face of the head was flat except for the valve ports. The effect was a fully machined combustion chamber that not only ensured all six were the same size - by no means common practice in the 1920s - but also smoothed out flame travel. Burning the mixture evenly, Poppe believed, was the secret of smooth running.

The Light Six sportsman's saloon, sometimes known as the Blue Train car, sported a hinged cover for the dumb-irons scooped out in the middle, and cycle-type wings of the sort that distinguished Aston Martin sports cars of the 1930s.

Unfortunately Poppe's reputation was in decline. Rover looked indecisive with both the 10/25 and the 16/50 still in production. Although there was little wrong with the cars, such proliferation was not the right policy for the intense competition at the close of the 1920s.

The Autocar road test of December 27, 1929, was astute enough to acknowledge the principal virtues of the Light Six, including good fuel consumption, which it put down to the low frontal area or 'small head resistance', as it was called.

Something of a pioneer design as one of the first relatively small saloons with a 2-litre six-cylinder engine, 'Light' Six still meant a weight of 25.5cwt and a four-seater two-door fabric saloon body only 13ft 3in long.

'There was a noticeable drone from the exhaust,' according to *The Autocar*, which was able to record a top speed of approximately 70mph *'under favourable conditions, that is with a good length of straight to run up to it, for the topmost limit is not reached quickly. A cruising speed of 50mph suited the car very well.'* Following a number of hill climb tests, during which a gradient of 1 in 10.5

approached at 55mph was crested at 30mph in top gear and a 1 in 6 needed first gear, the testers concluded that the car *'... is geared a shade high'*.

The advantage of high gearing was a fuel consumption of over 30mpg and relatively low engine speeds in long-distance cruising, which must have given Dudley Noble the confidence to organise the famous race with the Blue Train. The 0-50mph time was 41 sec.

Nearly half the wheelbase of the Light Six was occupied by the bonnet and scuttle, *'...and the back seats of the necessarily compact body overhang the rear wheels considerably'*. The Autocar was impressed with the instruments, *'separately sunk into a wooden facia board illuminated by a barrel-type dashlamp with, on either side of the facia board, a light luggage shelf'*.

It was a well-furnished car, with a screen wiper and *'...a tasteful and well-equipped interior, even to the provision of a separate ashtray for each passenger. The armrests of the rear seat*

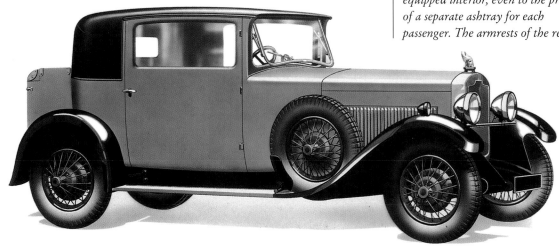

A two-year guarantee was offered with the 1928 Sportsman's Coupé at £425 (left)

In 1930 'Meteor' was appended to the Viking ship radiator badge (right)

are hollow and form small lockers, the tools are carried under the front seats, cords render the door locks easy to open from inside and the two large windows work with quick lift levers. There are deep wells for the legs of the rear seat passengers while the back squab is hinged at the top and, when opened, discloses the battery, a compartment for luggage, and a trap through which the reserve petrol tap can be reached.'

Searle knew he would be unable to recruit talent to a company as feeble as Rover without restoring morale, so Noble was instructed to put on a brave face. Favourable press comment was indispensable to Searle's plan, so Noble arranged for journalists to cover the International Six Days motorcycle trial in the Lake District, at the wheels of Light Sixes.

The car was displayed on the Rover stand at the 1928 Olympia motor show, and the press became so well disposed to it that Searle was able to persuade Spencer Wilks to take the job of general manager.

The Rovers now in production were the 16/50, with an enlarged version of the Poppe overhead cam four-cylinder, and the little Hillman-bodied Wilks-inspired 10/25. Searle discontinued the 16/50 and sold off the old stock, and the Ten with an enlarged version of the four-cylinder 9/20 of 1924 became one of the firm's main product lines. Poppe's six-cylinder engine

Rover advertising extolled the virtues of freewheeling in 1933. '*A child can make perfect clutchless changes*' it promised, in this Rover Ten Special Saloon. (left)

inaugurated a series of cars that saw Rover through the crisis. It was the basis of the Light Six 2-litre and Light Twenty 2.5-litre Meteor which, with a variety of bodies, formed the mainstay of the range until Wilks was able to introduce what came to be known as the P1 in 1934.

Meanwhile the Rover Ten four-cylinder was also developed into a six. Wilks commissioned a former colleague at Hillman, Major H B Thomas, to design a smaller 1.4-litre six-cylinder engine to fill the gap beneath the 2- and 2.6-litre renderings of Poppe's. Time and money were tight, so Thomas took the Rover Ten engine, added a couple of cylinders, changed the dimensions and produced a rather languid little power unit for the Rover Pilot produced in 1932-1933.

It was increased to 1.6-litres in an effort to provide something more than 35bhp, and ran smoothly enough on its four-bearing crankshaft. Introduced in the autumn of 1931 for the 1932 model year, the Pilot also felt the influence of Rover's new chief engineer, Maurice Wilks. He added a freewheel, and in the autumn of 1932 introduced another variant of the Pilot, the Speed Fourteen. This featured an underslung chassis and a 1,577cc tuned engine with three carburettors and sports exhaust. It produced 54bhp, a lively performance and a top speed of 80mph. A freewheel was not unique, but over the next 30 years it became

associated with silence, refinement, clutchless gearchanging - and Rover.

It was controlled by a knurled wheel on the dash; turning it to the right brought the freewheel into operation. To change up, the driver lifted his foot off the throttle and changed gear deliberately and slowly. A four-second pause was recommended - any shorter and the gears could grate. Changing down was easier and faster, and keeping the throttle slightly open helped the engine and road speeds synchronise. In use, the Bowden wire control tended to stretch, which was irksome to put right. The car had to be locked in gear, and the backlash on the control wheel taken up by an adjuster, with a locknut behind the instrument panel.

Despite this occasional drawback, the freewheel remained a popular feature on Rovers until the mid-1950s.

The Speed Fourteen influenced the shape and style of Rovers for twenty years. Its underslung chassis, planned for the range due in 1934, followed industry custom of inaugurating a feature on an expensive model and applying it to cheaper ones later. Its chassis frame was 6in longer than the standard Pilot and the side members swept under, not over, the rear axle. The goal was a long, low sporty body with a low centre of gravity to improve the handling.

Rover was making its way towards a distinctive appearance. Spencer Wilks felt it was important for cars to look right as well as feel right, and the Speed Pilot's extra length allowed a coupé appearance, while maintaining headroom in the rear. Rover lost no time in advertising a two-door coupé, with long sweeping wings and an integrated boot, made by Carbodies of Coventry.

COACH-BUILT SALOON, £435

The Rover line emerges. The rounded roof, the covered spare wheel on the boot lid, and the elegance of a small Bentley were hallmarks of the Hastings Coupé. (right)

THE "SPEED FOURTEEN" HASTINGS COUPE

THE Hastings Coupe takes its name from the R.A.C. 1,000 miles Rally held at Hastings, when it gained the highest award in its class—the Championship Cup, and also first prize in its individual classification.

The interior is upholstered in Vaumol hide, in a wide choice of colours. The rear seat has armrests at each side and a central folding armrest. The rear quarter window is hinged and made to open providing additional ventilation. The doors are wide and the floor level is low allowing easy entrance to both front and rear seats, and nothing is left out of the equipment which would contribute to comfort and convenience.

Equipment : Chromium plated head and side lamps, headlamps special Bi-flex fitted dip and switch, electric dual windscreen wipers, centrally controlled windscreen, sliding roof, built-in direction indicators, electric alto horn, trip speedometer, clock, revolution counter, ammeter, combined electric petrol and oil gauge, ignition switch, interior light, concealed instrument panel lights, driving mirror, ash trays, pile carpets, rope pulls, tinted glass rear window, interior sun visor, door louvres, rear stop lamp, fog lamp, reversing light, harmonic stabiliser, bumper at front, spare wheel and tyre, spare wheel cover and disc, centre fixing wheels, tool kit housed in tool tray under bonnet.

The built-in luggage compartment of the Hastings Coupe body on the "Speed Fourteen" and "Speed Twenty" chassis is considerably more commodious than is usual in a car of this type. Ample room is provided for suit cases and if required the lid of the compartment can be used as an extension.

THE "SPEED FOURTEEN" HASTINGS COUPE £395

It was called 'close-coupled', which meant there was not much legroom in the back. It was a style for which a later generation would invent new titles such as 2+2 or occasional four-seater, and it became significant for Rover following two coachwork awards in the 1933 RAC 1,000 Miles Rally at Hastings.

Rover also won the rally competition class for 16hp cars, in a tie-break from Donald Healey in his Invicta, a combination that won the Monte Carlo Rally two years before.

Yet it was the coachwork competition accompanying the rally at Hastings that ignited the fortunes of the company in the 1930s, just as

neighbouring Bexhill set the ball rolling in 1904.

Carbodies made Morris bodies as well, but it scarcely seemed to matter. Rover introduced the beautifully proportioned style as the Hastings Coupé, a new model with a brochure that said: '*The interior is upholstered in Vaumol hide in a wide choice of colours. The rear seat has armrests at both sides and a central folding armrest. The rear quarter window is hinged and made to open, providing additional ventilation. The doors are wide, and the floor level is low allowing easy entrance to both front and rear seats, and nothing is left out of the equipment which would contribute to comfort and convenience.*

'*Equipment: chromium plated head and side lamps, special Bi-flex headlamps with dip and switch, electric dual windscreen wipers, centrally controlled windscreen, safety glass all round, sliding roof, built-in direction indicators, electric alto horn, trip speedometer, clock, revolution counter, ammeter, combined electric petrol and oil gauge, ignition switch, interior light, concealed instrument panel lights, driving mirror, ash trays, pile carpets, rope pulls, tinted rear window, interior sun visor, door louvres, rear stop lamp, fog lamp, reversing light, harmonic stabiliser bumper at front, spare wheel and tyre, spare wheel cover and disc, centre fixing wheels, tool kit housed in tool tray under bonnet. Speed Fourteen Hastings Coupé, price £395.*'

Special bodies were not unusual when cars still had a strong separate chassis, and although custom-made strictly one-off affairs remained the province of Rolls-Royce, Daimler or Bentley buyers, the limited-production specialist designs for the likes of Rover were popular. Jaguar began life as the Swallow Sidecar and Coachbuilding Company, making a range of bodies for mounting on Morris Cowley, Austin Seven, Wolseley or Fiat chassis. Rover specialist body makers included Salmons of Newport Pagnell, which made substantial-looking open coupés with tops known as Tickford heads, and Midland Light Motor Bodies, which made the Melba four-door open tourer.

Coachbuilt middle-class cars did not survive the Depression. Mass-produced bodies so improved in quality and style that by the middle of the 1930s they were rare, and by the end they were almost extinct.

The Hastings Coupé became a catalogued model on the Speed Fourteen and Speed Twenty chassis, even though the larger car kept the obsolescent upswept rear axle, restricting headroom in the back. It was an uncommon car; only 204 were made in 1933. Yet it was Rover's flagship and was well received by road testers, who praised the handling and roadholding, together with the Lockheed hydraulic brakes.

There was clearly something about the cut of the Carbodies design that struck a chord with the Wilks brothers. It seemed to epitomise the tasteful middle-class precepts to which they aspired. It was not too fancy, the roof blended smoothly into the rear boot and there was a distinctive curve to the wings. The neat optional metal cover over the spare wheel looked practical and dignified, and the proportions and mouldings and upright radiator gave a hint of how Derby Bentleys would look two or three years later.

'*The doors are wide*', said the sales brochure. '*The low floor level allows easy entrance to both front and rear seats, and the built-in luggage compartment is considerably more commodious than usual for a car of this type.*' There was a useful amount of room for suitcases, and if there was not enough with the boot closed, it could remain open.

The lid opened flat to form a platform, something like the fold-out luggage grids of older cars, and the trunks or cases for a family holiday were strapped on. Too many spoilt the weight distribution, but with a full load performance was curtailed anyway, so the effect on handling was generally inconsequential.

The Hastings interior aspired to a degree of luxury, with pile carpet, ashtrays, braided rope pulls for passengers to hang on by, and a sun visor. Wealthy customers determined to make an impression could have a tinted rear window to keep the inside cool in hot weather, and an opening windscreen - essential for finding the

way through the frequent London fogs. An opening rear quarter-light improved ventilation, and there was a reversing lamp, a stop lamp and a fog lamp. A rev counter and the customary Rover combined petrol and oil-level gauge were standard, together with Trafficators, direction indicator arms that stuck out and lit up.

Rover's commitment to its owner-drivers was subtle. It took care to involve them in the running of the car almost as amateur engineers, providing them with professional-looking tool kits and an oil-level reading on the fuel gauge. An oil-level gauge was another Rover feature that lingered well into the 1960s.

Selling cars to the fastidious middle class meant a wide selection of body styles. Rover's range was as wide as the grand titles and descriptions inherited from the bespoke carriage trade. Snobbery was implicit not only in names echoing the Raj, but in calling windows 'lights'. 'Fixed-head' simply meant that the fabric-covered coupé-like roof did not open up. Fastbacks known as Streamline Coupés were based on Fourteen and Speed Fourteen chassis with echoes of Chrysler Airflow, art deco and faired-in railway locomotives.

The explanation for the Hastings Coupé being made close-coupled was that it brought the rear seat ahead of the axle, putting the passengers within the wheelbase and making them lower and more comfortable. It also left room for a new luxury, an enclosed luggage boot.

Rover's traditional pattern of well-sprung leather seats, and polished wood for the dashboard and window surrounds, emerged with the Hastings Coupé. There was a blind for the rear window to prevent dazzle from following headlights (and perhaps give Betjeman's subaltern a bit of privacy in the Camberley car park), a sliding sunshine roof, a parcel net in the ceiling and pile carpets.

Some Speed Fourteen Sports Tourers were made as jaunty open four-seaters with cutaway doors. They were more refined than most sports cars of the period, although less fast, and no more than 150 were made between 1933 and 1936.

By the time *The Autocar* tested a 12hp Pilot Six Saloon on August 28, 1931, Rover was getting back on course. Testers and customers alike appreciated the car's refinement and quietness: '*According to its makers the new Rover 12hp six-cylinder Pilot is intended to be a vehicle of about the 10hp size but possessed of greater refinement. A test of the new car showed that this claim is perfectly justified - it has a very definite fascination. For the engine is as smooth, quiet and sweet-running as anyone could desire. It is even above the*

average for a good small Six. The charm of the Pilot - and there is charm - does not lie in a snappy performance, but in a willing gentleness to perform every task neatly and without fuss.'

Rover's gift for matching the car to the market was showing through again: '*It is particularly to the taste of those who like comfortable quiet travelling with no dawdling by the wayside but no hurry. The engine exerts its power with an air so modest as to be deceptive, remembering that it is less than 1.5 litres in capacity yet is pulling a full-sized metal-panelled four-seater saloon body.*

'*The Pilot managed 42mph in third gear, and was commended for being able to proceed at walking pace in top gear, with no need to manipulate the ignition lever to avoid pinking.'* Yet there was some faint praise as well, with one of *The Autocar*'s discreetly worded reprimands: '*Remembering that the car is not an expensive one, the indirect gears may be regarded as unexpectedly quiet, and the silent third as sufficiently silent.'*

'Sufficiently' in this case probably meant 'insufficiently'.

Publicity stunts were still not quite Rover's style, and would be proscribed once the tactful Wilks was in charge, but sales promotion was needed, and Dudley Noble was called in by Frank Searle and Spencer Wilks to put the

cars before the public. Noble's best opportunity lay with the speedy and comely Light Six even though its sales were modest. It was more likely to get into the papers than a dull Rover.

"*I want to see it splashed in a national daily,*" Searle told Noble. "*Something that will make people talk.*" What he really wanted was free publicity to augment Rover's modest advertising budget, which amounted to a page once a month in the *Daily Mail* (circulation 2,000,000 - whole page £900 or £1,200 for the front), the *Daily Express*, and the *Manchester Daily Dispatch*.

Early fastback. (above) The vogue for streamlining in the 1930s produced one of the first smooth-tailed body styles, the Speed Fourteen.

Harold Pemberton, motoring corrrespondent of the Daily Express, modestly omitted his role in the Blue Train story reproduced by Rover advertising.
(right)

the Blue Train, but by the implied affinity with them, some of their celebrity status was bound to rub off.

The Blue Train was made up of blue-painted luxury sleeping and restaurant cars, and departed from Calais quay on the arrival of the 11am service from Victoria to Dover. It connected with what Noble called the Southern Railways crack mailboat across the Channel.

The departure from Calais was 2.30 '...*or as soon as the nobility and gentry had settled down in their Pullmans. It was the quintessence of gracious travel in an era when the French Riviera and Monte Carlo were the wintertime goal of all those in the social swim.*'

It took close on 24 hours for the train to reach its terminus at Ventimille (Ventimiglia) just over the Italian border from Menton.

'*Most people imagined that it travelled at nearly a mile a minute*,' wrote Noble. '*I did too until careful investigation of the timetable revealed that its average speed from start to finish was some 40mph. This was because its passage round Paris on the ceinture railway from the Gare du Nord to the Gare de Lyon wasted nearly three-quarters of an hour. It also stopped at Dijon for a change of locomotive, and at Marseille went into a dead end and came out with a fresh engine in the reverse direction.*'

Racing the Blue Train had been in Noble's mind for some time. '*It was a train that conveyed the wealthy or high-born away from the English winter, to the sunnier clime of the* French and Italian Riviera.' It seemed to symbolise the style to which Rover was trying to aspire. There may not have been a single Rover customer among the high-born blue-bloods on

Beating it to the Riviera was, accordingly, only a matter of driving at a good speed without too many stops.

Noble's idea was accepted with alacrity once Searle realised that three people's expenses for a week, plus petrol and cross-Channel fares, would amount to less than £100. Noble approached Harold Pemberton, motoring correspondent of the *Daily Express,* who obtained the approval of the editor, Beverley Baxter, and the scheme was put into operation.

It was fraught with difficulties. Noble's wife died of TB on January 10, 1930, ten days before the expedition set off. Yet on the 20th Pemberton and Noble, accompanied by a factory test driver, Frank Bennett, crossed the Channel, stayed the night in Calais, and braced themselves for a long drive.

They photographed the car beside the Blue Train locomotive at a level crossing on the quayside, from which they could make their getaway on to Route Nationale 1. The mailboat arrived and the engine's whistle showed that the train was about to leave.

'*At the first puff from the smoke stack we were aboard the car with engine running and first gear engaged. We made our way at all speed out of the dock area, through the town and on to the main road in the direction of Boulogne, Abbeville and Beauvais.*'

They avoided Paris and with daylight fading forged on south, into the wooded country round Fontainebleau. A halo round the headlamps of oncoming cars was the first sign of evening mist, and by 8 o'clock it was foggy. They still had an hour in hand over the train, but by 3am when the little Rover reached Chalons-sur-Saône, the driver was being guided only by the street lights. In the thickening gloom they were forced to stop after covering 300 miles in twelve hours.

By morning the fog had gone but so had the Blue Train. There was nothing for it but to carry on to the Riviera, and try again on the way back. They drove the rest of the way to Nice with only one stop at Brignôles. On Sunday they set off again, this time from St Raphael in heavy rain and darkness. After only about 30 miles, Bennett misjudged a sharp bend and the car plunged off the road into a field about ten feet below. Pemberton was knocked unconscious but the crew was otherwise unscathed. It took an hour to get the car back on the road damaged and barely driveable. The nearside wing was bent back on to the wheel, so clearly there would be no more racing of trains that night.

The party stayed at Brignôles again, and in the morning Bennett repaired

The Rover Light Six waiting at a British railway station. (left)

the wing and a broken silencer. Back at St Raphael another Blue Train set off. This time the weather was clear, and the Rover reached the Gare Maritime in Calais with 20 minutes to spare. Pemberton's story, datelined Calais, January 28, 1930, made a front-page lead in the *Daily Express.*

The model subsequently gained stronger attachments for the front wings, which were bolted racily to the brake back plates and steered with the wheels. By the time the team made it back to Calais, both wings had broken off at the attachments.

Racing the Blue Train, like the race to bring the first Beaujolais Nouveau to London, reached epidemic proportions. On February 24, an Alvis Silver Eagle beat the express by three hours, covering one stretch of 112 miles in two hours.

The exploit was repeated by the charismatic Woolf Barnato to show how easily it could be done in a Bentley. Barnato needed the publicity too; Bentley was on the brink of receivership and he was the managing director.

Barnato set off with a golfing friend not from the railway station at Cannes, but from the bar at the Carlton. They awaited word that the Blue Train had departed, finished their drinks, and left for an exploit that, like Rover's, went down in automotive folklore. The car

was a Bentley Speed Six with a long, tall bonnet and sweeping roofline.

It set a trend that Rover would soon follow. Barnato and the coachbuilder Gurney Nutting had invented the fastback. Largest in the Rover range, the 20hp Meteor had a Treasury rating of 19.3hp, which made the annual tax £20. The Speed model had a high-geared 3.7:1 instead of the standard 4.7:1 axle and *The Autocar* was impressed when it achieved a top speed of 88.33mph and braked to a stop from 30mph in 31ft. Meteor production stopped in mid-1933 although derivatives were still catalogued for 1934.

The Meteor could be supplied with a Bendix automatic clutch to make driving easier. The inlet manifold depression furnished the energy for a servo cylinder to work the clutch, providing a sort of two-pedal control. Rover claimed it improved petrol and oil consumption, produced less wear on the transmission, and the automatic freewheel made hill starts less of an effort.

With the engine idling, the depression held the clutch out of engagement. When the driver engaged gear and pressed the accelerator, the servo no longer held the clutch out, but let it in against its springs. A locking button by the driver's idle foot brought the clutch back to normal operation, because once under way, when the

driver lifted his foot off the throttle the clutch disengaged. This was all very well as a means of bringing in the freewheel, but it was not to every driver's taste. If the engine stalled, the inlet depression re-engaged the clutch, which then automatically restarted the engine again on compression.

The Pilot and the Meteor were interim Rovers, filling the hiatus between the unruly 1920s and the well-ordered and more prosperous years of the 1930s. Rover was still searching for a role, and despite the attainments of the Meteor and Pilot and the high visibility of the Light Six, that had been elusive.

Now, at the dawn of the new decade, a new management was in place to crystallise policy and press forward with cars that would put Rover firmly into a niche it would occupy for succeeding generations.

Drivers of cars with the new four-wheel brakes hoped to avoid collisions from behind by warning followers of their efficiency. (right)

CHAPTER IV

Wilks Masterpieces

I n 1931 Rover was emerging from crisis. The slump struck the motor industry hard, especially firms making middle-class cars, and the proliferation of models from the Pilot to the Meteor was unsatisfactory. Rover's range, from a Family Ten to a large limousine costing almost £600, was not only uneconomic in view of the production numbers, but dictated too wide a range of engineering and componentry than a small firm could deal with.

The reconstitution of the board came early in 1932, and with Searle gone Spencer Wilks finally took control.

Once again Rover expected that harsh times would lead to a demand for economy cars and underwent the classic reaction of car makers to economic downturns. The flat-twin Eight, made in the 1920s, had done well, although in the end it proved no match for the Austin Seven. Rover saw no reason why history should not repeat itself, and planned an unconventional rear-engined air-cooled V-twin with independent suspension, to sell at £89.

It was a hopeless mistake, but examined in the clear light of hindsight it must have seemed logical enough. The slump was an international imbroglio and Rover was not alone in thinking about a small economy car. A German technical journalist and spirited advocate of rear engines was thinking along the same lines. Josef Ganz first proposed an economy car, with a two-cylinder engine and swing-axle independent springing, in 1923, and designed one for Zündapp, the Nüremberg motorcycle manufacturers.

It had a backbone frame, and a prototype was made in 1929 with a tiny 175cc motorcycle engine and chain drive. Spurned, Ganz turned to Adler, which ordered another prototype, and then to Daimler-Benz. But like the French Claveau and Guerin, the Italian San Giusto and a Dornier of 1924, it came to nothing. It was left to Ferdinand Porsche to pick up the pieces not only of Ganz's failures, but also the rear-engined Mercedes-Benz experiments and Edmund Rumpler's streamliner of 1929, and create the Volkswagen. Rover's contribution to the vogue for

Wings on the Viking's helmet were blown back by the speed of the 1930s (left) that began in the wintry wind of a slump. (right)
Rover 10/25 family saloon of 1931 sold for £189 with safety glass windscreen.

rear-engined air-cooled cars was the Scarab. Its plans were shrouded in secrecy until September 1931, when the car was revealed at a publicity lunch given by Henlys, the London distributor.

A prototype was displayed, but close inspection forbidden, probably because it was still incomplete. What was conspicuous was a simple motorcycle air-cooled pushrod overhead valve Vee-twin engine at the rear, open four-seater bodywork, and a rather self-conscious dummy Rover radiator and cycle-type wings. The wings followed the lines of the Blue Train Light Six although they did not turn with the wheels. Many details of the Scarab remained sketchy, because the drawings were lost during the war and none of the prototypes survived.

The proportions were good. The Scarab had a louvred tail, like the Volkswagen, and followed some of the other precepts subsequently adopted by Porsche. The cylinders measured 75mm x 95mm making the engine 839cc, and aluminium was used for the crankcase and pistons. The Vee configuration suited the circular sweep of a cooling fan, since no formal air ducting was planned. There was a roller bearing crankshaft and the oil pump was driven off the distributor drive-shaft. Suspension at the front was by sliding pillars with duplex springs, of the sort adopted by Morgan and Lancia. The rear was a prophetic

swing-axle arrangement pivoted above the gearbox, with coil springs and widely spaced wishbones. The brakes were inboard drums alongside the final drive.

Ferdinand Porsche and Dr Hans Nibel of Daimler-Benz came to examine the suspension, apparently in the course of protecting Porsche's patent rights, and reported that the car handled well. They seemed surprised at the understeer they encountered at a time when they were trying to eradicate terminal oversteer (tail-heaviness) in their designs.

According to a memoir by Edward Eves, Midland Editor of *The Autocar*, they failed to appreciate the significance of the chassis designer Frank Searle's rear spring balance arm,

which took rear roll stiffness out of the car, giving it the pronounced understeer that eluded them.

Rover thought it could make 30,000 Scarabs a year, and a dozen prototypes gave no more than the customary teething troubles expected from such a radical design. Production plans were put in hand and a brochure produced.

Design work began in September 1929 and continued for two years before Wilks cancelled it following Searle's departure.

Once again an obsession with breaking into the volume market proved to be Rover's undoing, with Searle and the chairman, W D Sudbury, hoping the Scarab would take Rover into the popular domain.

Rover's radical rear-engined runabout of 1931 never reached production. (above)

Ferdinand Porsche was impressed with the handling of rear-engined prototype. (below)

Rover 10/25 saloons at the factory gate in 1931. (right) Electric windscreen wiper on the driver's side and a folding luggage grid were standard, wire wheels £5 extra.

Rover was still a small-quantity producer of 3,500 cars a year and Sudbury and Searle were tempted by Morris's 55,000 and Austin's 25,000 into believing Rover could follow suit. Robert Boyle and Maurice Wilks worked on the Scarab in secret at Searle's home at Braunston. The wheelbase was 84in (4in longer than a Mini), the chassis simple, and the 60-degree engine cooled by a two-bladed fan. The body was ash framed and there was seating for four on thinly upholstered chairs.

Senior staff who experienced the rough and noisy engine were offended, and unconvinced about its rear location despite the enthusiasm shown by theoretical engineers such as Ganz. Major Thomas was commissioned to design a front-engined front-wheel-drive alternative, just in case a new small car was inescapable.

Having disposed of Searle, Wilks decided that the investment was out of proportion to the profits the Scarab could have generated. Rover spent £10,000 on it, £5,000 was set aside for early tooling, but a further £50,000 was needed before it could be made. A car was shown at Olympia and kindled little interest, and by the time of the Glasgow motor show barely three weeks later it had passed into history.

With notable exceptions such as the Austin Seven and Sir Alec Issigonis's Mini, projects undertaken under the pressure of economic hardship were often ill-judged or short-lived. Hard times bred cyclecars and bubble cars, neither of which had distinguished careers, following crises such as the first world war and Suez in the 1950s.

History may be harsh in judging the Scarab a failure, for it must have seemed a legitimate initiative at the time, especially in view of rear-engined cars planned elsewhere. But Rover was not the best size to make a small car in large numbers. The sums did not add up; besides Wilks had better things on his mind.

By 1934 his philosophy was becoming clear. The P1, not the Scarab, was his prescription for Rover's recovery. Spencer and his brother both understood good taste, or what they thought the British middle class regarded as good taste. They wanted quality, reliability, longevity and refinement; they were shrewd judges.

Unlike their predecessors they were more interested in making small production runs of premium-priced cars than big numbers like Austin and Morris for the mass market. Some of Rover's immediate middle-class competitors such as Lanchester and Humber, Armstrong-Siddeley and Alvis went down different roads - Humber was absorbed by the Rootes group, Lanchester and Daimler by BSA, Alvis and Armstrong-Siddeley drove upmarket, survived the war, but went on to extinction in the 1960s.

Spencer Wilks's acumen was amply demonstrated in his next brief to technical director Maurice Wilks and chief designer Robert Boyle. He asked them for an engine that could be adapted for the new Ten and Twelve. The resulting Wilks/Boyle creation came to be known as the 100mm engine from the length of its stroke. Its capacity for different cars was varied by altering the bore. The benefits became clear as production engineering emerged as one of the motor industry's

The ROVER
"SPEED FOURTEEN"
Streamline Four-Door Coupe

higher sciences. The cylinder blocks went through the same machines; the only real difference was the setting on the tool that cut the cylinder bores.

Two four-cylinder units went into production first, with a six-cylinder planned for a Fourteen and a Sixteen when the market recovered from the depressed 1930s. Rubber engine mountings damped out vibration as

Rover took another step towards achieving the quietness and refinement so close to Spencer Wilks's heart.

The P1 Ten, Twelve and Fourteen were the three models in the 1934 programme. They were the first popular production Rovers with underslung frames, overhead-valve engines, and a freewheel in the transmission.

The Ten had the Wilks/Boyle 100mm four-cylinder engine with a 66.5mm bore giving a capacity of 1,389cc, and sold for £238. The first Rover Twelve since 1932 had a 69mm bore and sold for £268, while the Fourteen inherited the old Thomas-designed 1,577cc six-cylinder version of the 1923 four, and went on sale at £288.

The style of the cars was upright, with

the well-known slatted grille with its strong central spine, and the triangular Viking ship badge first used in 1929. The entire range had the harmonic front bumper designed to stabilise the car on its springs. Wilmot-Breeden, the accessory firm, developed it to compensate for the frame stiffness lost when flexible engine mountings were introduced. It was, in effect, a transverse leaf spring with heavy bob-weights on each end, and remained a feature of British middle-class saloons well into the 1940s, when stiffer chassis frames rendered it unnecessary.

The Autocar verified its effectiveness by removing one from a Fourteen saloon to discover what the car was like undamped. The chassis-twisting effects of rough roads made it squirm uncomfortably. During a materials shortage following the second world war, these unusual stabilising bumpers were omitted from some cars. The chassis jiggle was acceptable on British roads, but proved so severe in export markets still with pavé roads that an emergency programme of reinstating them had to be put in hand.

Rover's and Wilmot-Breeden's bumper was not the only patent gadget to be found on Rovers. The Lucas Startix system fitted to the P1 was for restarting a stalled engine automatically. The starter was actuated if the dynamo stopped charging, an ingenious piece of automation for the 1930s, but inconvenient if the dynamo

Rover Speed Fourteen of 1935. (left)

Maximum speed recorded by *The Autocar* - 82.57mph; 0-60mph acceleration - 21.4sec.

Bumper badge (above)

Strong headlights, windtone horns, and pass-lamp essential for high-speed touring (right)

Southampton as the
Queen Mary prepares for
her maiden voyage in May
1936. (left)
'*Two outstanding examples
of British engineering*'
according to Rover. Car
14hp 6-cylinder sports
saloon, £318. Fare to
New York - from £37.

stopped charging for a reason other than a stalled engine. A broken fan belt was not unusual.

In these circumstances the starter tried to engage a running engine with destructive consequences. The system had a three-way switch, and drivers had to remember to leave the gear lever in neutral when the device was engaged. Switching over to automatic,

with the car in gear, set off the starter and the car would move off on its own. Lucas introduced a vacuum safety switch as a counter-measure, but Rover abandoned the system in 1936.

Convenience gadgetry knew no bounds, and for 1935 P1 models Rover followed the example of Rolls-Royce and Alvis, with automatic chassis lubrication. Maintenance was a

pressing problem when grease guns had to be applied with great frequency to lubricate the suspension, steering, brakes and transmission. There were no oil-less bushes or sealed-for-life joints. Moving parts such as spring leaves and shackles had to be lubricated, or they wore out and failed, or else produced more squeaks and rattles than Rover owners felt they deserved. Service intervals for some greasing points could be as short as a few hundred miles or every week. All very well in the days of the chauffeur but bothersome for the new non-technical generation of owner-driver.

Many remedies were tried. Rover adopted the Luvax-Bijur system, as fitted to the Belgian Minerva, in which a reservoir on the bulkhead was linked to a network of small-bore brass tubes. Once a day, or at intervals of 100 miles or so, the driver pressed a plunger and a combination of springs and air pressure supplied the energy which, all being well, piped oily fluid to 23 lubrication points.

Brake cross shafts, road springs, steering links, swivel pins and handbrake linkages were among the destinations for the eggcupful of oil released through valves calibrated to supply each point with what was needed. The process took several minutes and, it seemed, might do away with one of motoring's major chores.

Arterial occlusions proved the system's undoing. To make things worse, difficulties generally came to light only when lack of lubrication caused failures. Tending grease nipples proved to be easier than keeping arteriosclerosis at bay, and although Rover persevered with it until 1947, central lubrication proved better in theory than in practice. Once modern technical alternatives were devised, it was gratefully dropped.

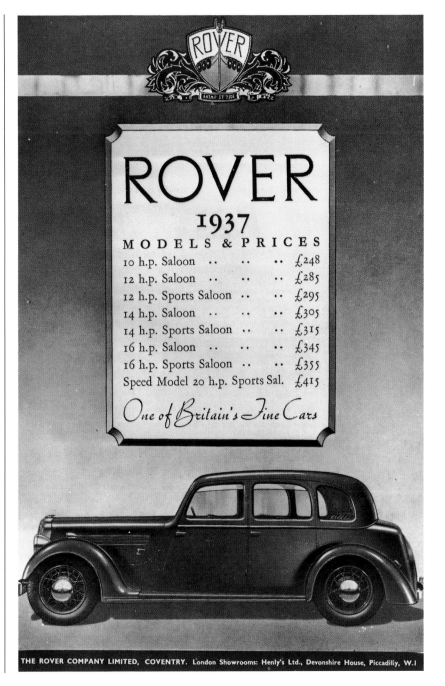

The Fourteen inherited the existing six-cylinder engine and the Speed Fourteen's extended underslung chassis. There were new four-speed constant-mesh gearboxes with helical-toothed second and third gears to reduce whine. The sales brochures were obliged to refer to the indirect gears as 'silent' to keep abreast of rivals using similar euphemisms.

The 100mm engine proved such a success that for 1935 the Fourteen's old 1,577cc unit needed a higher compression ratio and airflowed ports to give it sufficient power to stay ahead of the 1,496cc Twelve. It also obtained three extra inches on the wheelbase, to sustain the difference and justify the extra cost.

Ambitious plans to develop the 100mm engine formula into a six-cylinder reached fruition in due course, and Maurice Wilks contemplated V-6 and V-8 variants as well. Anticipating the late-1930s rationalisation programme, already twenty years ahead of its time, Wilks saw the possibilities of a variety of modular engines fitting into one basic chassis.

Working under Maurice Wilks, Jack Swaine drew up two new engines. They were a 60-degree V-8 and a 90-degree V-6 with a single camshaft in the middle and overhead inlet and side exhaust valves. The apparently eccentric V-angles were explained by Swaine as expediency in the face of

carburation difficulties with the two-plane crank of the V-8.

The proposition that a V-8 was only two four-cylinder engines working on a common crankcase, and a V-6 was much the same with two cylinders deleted, unfortunately miscarried. The V-8 was never made, and although a prototype of the six-cylinder was tried, it was never put into production.

The effort was by no means wasted. The sloping-head inlet-over-exhaust (ioe) layout that Swaine adopted to keep the engine narrow enough for the slim engine bays of pre war cars, was revived in the late 1940s for the in-line engine of the P3. Maurice Wilks liked the efficient combustion chamber

shape, and an in-line version of it was running by 1939.

The Lockheed hydraulic brakes of the Speed Fourteen were not carried forward to the new Ten and Twelve. They made do with Girling rod-operated mechanical brakes, which were quite adequate for the modest performance. The Fourteen kept its hydraulics until 1936, when it too reverted to reliable, non-leak and smooth-operating rods.

A limited number of aluminium-bodied fastbacks was built in 1935-37, selling for £415. The engine had three carburettors, a high-compression cylinder head with airflowed ports, and 'sports' exhaust giving enough

Sport Rovers. Speed Fourteen of 1935. (left) and the four-seat Tickford drop-head coupé of 1938-1948. (right)

extra power to justify the modest increase in noise. A cruising speed of 70mph was claimed, and a top speed of 82mph. It had distinctive close-mounted headlights, and a racy-looking pass-lamp mounted on a chrome tripod, flanked by long windtone horns. Wire wheels with centrelock spinners and a Brooklands fishtail exhaust gave it the flavour of a contemporary Riley. Standard-colour paintwork remained a useful economy at Rover in 1934, when the entire range had black-painted wings whatever colour the body was. Two-tone colours came in for 1935 and streamlined bodies were only ever single-colour.

The second part of Spencer Wilks's plan was revealed with the new range for 1937. Rover was tidying up. The philosophy, the middle-class target customers, remained the same, but the mixture of body styles that emerged from the confusion of the early 1930s was rationalised. The racy speed models and tourers that sold only in small numbers were deleted, and two basic body styles were created to cover the market. Two new six-cylinder chassis were introduced, and family Rovers with a family resemblance were inaugurated, ranging from 12hp to 20hp. Bodies were six-light and four-light, the saloons more upright and taller than the coupé-style four-light, and the interiors further refined and better furnished.

Rover at home in the Cotswolds. Peacetime study of 1939 Rover Sixteen at Chedworth in Gloucestershire. (left)

The restyling of 1937, marking the arrival of the range that came to be known as P2, looked as though it owed something to the contemporary Mercedes-Benz. It gave Rover a distinctive appearance that lasted well into the 1950s, with rounded wings and a strong waistline running into the rear luggage boot, a practical hangover from the Hastings Coupé of 1933. The boot with the spare wheel in the drop-down lid was now a boxy compartment capable of holding good-sized suitcases, and a useful advance on the external grid on which luggage was exposed to rain and smut.

One of the virtues, from Rover's standpoint, of the British middle-class market was its conservatism. It distrusted change. It wanted its cars and its standards and its Betjemanesque qualities to remain the same, if not for ever, then at least for as far as it could see ahead. Wilks turned this to advantage. Rover achieved an enduring body style that remained in vogue for years. It was good business. It avoided unseemly fashion contests, it preserved good taste, and above all it was thrifty not to alter the body style too often.

The 10hp carried on for a further two years with the old chassis, engine and body. The Twelve and Fourteen chassis was carried forward but equipped with the new body style. The 14hp gained a 2-litre version of the 100mm engine. The 16hp and the 20hp acquired both a new chassis and a new body - the 20hp called at first the Speed Model - and two new versions of the 100mm engine. The wheelbase was fixed at 115in but the track of the bigger cars was an inch wider.

Rover dealers were invited to put their name to an advertisement demonstrating the fuel savings available to freewheelers.
(right)

Special Advertisement available as above (6″ × 2 cols.).

owners counted more than anything. Among the other quirky options in 1937 were two different sorts of spring-spoke steering wheel. Steering often reacted strongly through the wheel, especially on stiffly sprung sports cars, and sprung wheels were a popular accessory even on cars that did not have kick-back.

Buyers could specify a badge bar. Keen motorists in the 1930s joined car clubs, and badges that in years to come would be a target of souvenir hunters showed the clannish, clubby British at their best.

Rover also offered a cross-bar ahead of the radiator for what was known as a pass-lamp, an auxiliary light working in conjunction with non-dipping headlamps. Before sealed beams and efficient double filament dipping bulbs, the offside headlamp was extinguished, and the nearside reflector tilted by means of a solenoid to point the beam downwards. With a pass-lamp, the offside light still went out, but it was replaced by the downward-pointing beam of the central light, which did not dazzle drivers passing in the opposite direction - hence the term. The central light also served as a foglight.

A favourite luxury accessory, in an era when luggage boots were modestly dimensioned, was a set of fitted suitcases. Rover customers could also have a cigarette lighter, a twin-plug

Punctures were still a major worry in the 1930s, and the DWS built-in jacking system was an attempt to provide Rover customers with peace of mind. It hoisted the car clear of the ground, enabling a wheel to be changed, by means of hydraulic

pressure raised by pumping with a small handle found in the toolkit. It was expensive to instal, the hand-pump and the hydraulic plungers under the chassis needed frequent maintenance, and it tended to leak when it grew old. But the reassurance it offered Rover

inspection lamp socket and a master battery switch, knock-on wire wheels or a compact Philips radio with an aerial mounted discreetly under the running board. Showy radio masts seemed vulgar and out of place in a Rover. Knock-on wire wheels were caddish too, and most owners preferred large discs covering the standard bolt-on wire wheels. This made them easier to clean in theory, but in practice meant they were hardly ever cleaned at all. The discs not only covered dirty wheels, but also made the car look more like the large formal saloons that Rover drivers so admired.

The 1937 Ten still had a reserve petrol tap under the boot floor, giving access to a spare gallon in the ten-gallon tank. The tap was later relocated to the dashboard. The main change for 1939 was the belated abandonment of the veteran 1,577cc engine for the Fourteen. This dated back to the 1928 Thomas-designed 10/25 and the Nizam, and the Pilot of 1932. It was replaced by another 100mm variant, the 1,901cc, Treasury rated at 14.9hp,

which meant it was taxed as a 15hp. The 1939 16hp cars had 2in extra on the rear track to provide a wider back seat, and Luvax piston-type shock absorbers to achieve a smoother ride. It was necessary to appeal to a generation beginning to appreciate the softness of American and Canadian cars. Not every wealthy motorist bought a Rolls-Royce and even the Prince of Wales, later Edward VIII, displayed a fondness for Canadian-made Buicks.

The 100mm four-cylinder engines gained an eight-port head, giving each cylinder its own breathing space, which together with a high compression ratio increased power. An interior heater was an extra-cost option.

Spencer Wilks's achievement was more than simply returning Rover to profit. By 1935 the accumulated debts were cleared, and production was up from the modest levels of 1933, when fewer than 5,000 cars were built, to more than 11,000 in 1939. Rover's share of the British market rose from 2.2 per cent to 3.2 per cent, and the company profit was a healthy £205,957. Competition was keen from the likes of Wolseley which, even though it was a badge-engineered Morris, managed to appeal to a genteel section of the middle-class priced a shade under the Rover. There was negligible threat from imported makes and little demand for exports, although Rovers

did find their way to far-flung outposts of Empire, in the hands of expatriates reluctant to relinquish a vehicle that epitomised a cherished way of life.

But the war clouds were gathering, and Betjeman's subaltern soon had a stern challenge to face.

Lines of the Hastings Coupé developed through the 1930s. Rear-hinged doors of the four-door were small, but so was the rear seat.
(left)

Rover 16 of Charlie Taylor, Stratford-upon-Avon.
(right)

CHAPTER V

Soaring Forties

The cars that went into production after the war were much the same as those Rover was making when the Helen Street factory was bombed on November 14, 1940. The Wilks brothers named them P1 for Postwar 1, but the title was only used by engineers and on internal management memos, and the 1939-1948 cars became known by their retrospective term of P2. They entered into a different world from the one surrendered in 1939, when the P2 was barely two seasons old. Shortage of materials, quota systems for supplies, steel allocations and a distorted market presented a fresh set of difficulties.

It was not a time for rancour. The afflictions were as nothing compared with the privations and tragedies of war-time, although working to the directions of a bureaucracy indifferent to the plight of a luxury car maker such as Rover was not easy.

Government permits were bestowed for the production of 500 10hp cars,

500 12hp cars and 100 six-cylinder cars - regarded by the incoming Labour administration as unnecessarily luxurious. Whitehall central planning would have preferred larger numbers of small cars, but Rover was not about to embark on a radical change, for the time being at any rate.

Production of Tens began before the end of 1945 and the first left-hand-drive models, for the 1947 model year, were Sixteens and Tens. Paintwork was black, the upholstery brown, although it was not long before colours were available to brighten the post-war gloom. The customers were mostly content with black, except for venturesome individuals who preferred maroon or dark green. Another ten years passed before Rover risked a production two-colour scheme.

Determined to show the government how seriously Rover was taking the export drive, Sir Stafford Cripps, the President of the Board of Trade, was invited to open the new Solihull factory freed from war-time

Two non-starters.
(above)
Fads not followed in the 1940s included a post-war prototype (top) and full width front with P3 rear.
(below)

P2 elegance; 1947 16 Sports Saloon, owned by John Millward of Leamington. Rover 16s had disc wheels and a Radiomobile antenna above the windscreen.
(left)

production on February 2, 1946. The new government regarded the motor industry with deep suspicion, as something of an indulgence even, in a world where producing necessities was a stern business.

Matters were worse in France, where a new tax discriminated against cars over 2.8 litres, a blow to the French luxury car industry from which it never recovered. Talbot, Delage, Delahaye and Hotchkiss perished, to France's everlasting disadvantage.

In Britain the basic petrol ration was reintroduced. In June 1945 it came as the first indication that war-time restrictions were at last being eased, and drivers were allowed about 200 miles (320km) a month. Petrol remained rationed until May 1950, and branded petrols did not reappear until 1953.

One measure introduced to pay for the war was purchase tax on cars, instituted in October 1940 at 33.3% of the ex-works wholesale price. This was doubled in June 1947, and the 66.6% rate lasted until April 1953. Up to 1951 it was levied on so-called luxury cars over £1,280; thereafter it applied to all until Heathcote Amory's budget of 1959 reduced it to 50%.

It was well into the 1950s before supply exceeded demand. The shortage of new cars led, in July

No one who drives the Rover Sixty or Seventy Five for the first time can easily forget the experience. Here are all the traditional smoothness and refinements so long associated with Rover cars, plus a new responsiveness which gives a fresh meaning to the words "One of Britain's Fine Cars". Yet despite their brilliant performance and remarkable flexibility these new Rover engines demand less fuel than their predecessors. Such is the result of high quality design.

ROVER

One of Britain's Fine Cars

Interim P3, the 75 introduced in 1948 with the overhead inlet valve engine.
(left)

1946, to a covenant scheme run by the Society of Motor Manufacturers and Traders (SMMT), with the government's encouragement. This was designed to foil speculators reaping large rewards from the premiums at which secondhand cars were selling. New car buyers promised to keep their car for six months, extended in March 1948 to a year, and finally in September 1950 to two years. Covenants did not end until cars became more or less freely available in 1953. Credit restrictions were introduced in February 1952 to curb the growing demand for cars.

Interiors in fine leather
and warm wood
characteristically
Rover.
(right)

The government stipulated a minimum deposit of 33.3% and the repayment period was limited to 18 months. In a seller's market, there was little incentive to make great changes to Rover's range, and Postwar 1 carried on until the end of 1947. Once a change had been decided on, tooling began for the P3's introduction the following February.

Among the modifications instituted for the first post-war Rovers were a Clayton-Dewandre heater, with an arrangement for blowing warm air to demist the windscreen, and an aperture in the facia to accommodate a radio.

In a rare concession to prodigality a 12 Tourer was introduced in 1947 supposedly, in the way things were, for export only. The entire production run was made with righthand drive so a number found their way on to the home market.

Mystery surrounds the motivation for the model. It was a singularly non-standard production, and the body followed the lines of a similar car of 1934-1936. Rover folklore suggests that since the relevant drawings and records were lost in the war, and Maurice Wilks was diffident about designing a new body style, a copy was made of a 1930s original bought back for the purpose. The hood folded away under a metal cover, a refinement for open cars rarely seen again until the 1980s.

Yet even the official government planners - especially the planners - could not overlook the necessity of preparing for the future. Rover was allowed to construct eight development or prototype vehicles.

The Ten, Twelve, Fourteen and Sixteen duly went back into production. The Twenty fell victim to the bureaucrats who directed Rover to build cars principally for export. Britain was impoverished by

the war, large cars were deemed unnecessary and unless Rover met its export quota obligations, steel allocations would be withdrawn in favour of companies that did. In 1948 George Strauss, the Minister of Supply, said that steel would be allocated only to firms which exported three-quarters of their output.

Such demands were not easy to fulfil since Rovers had never been designed for overseas markets. The company preferred to leave these to companies such as Standard, which had taken on the export drive with enthusiasm, but it was left with no choice.

If proof was ever needed that central direction of the motor industry was wasteful, inefficient and ultimately unsuccessful, it was available by 1950. The Ministry of Reconstruction decreed that the proliferation of models was wasteful, and encouraged manufacturers to concentrate on one apiece.

An analogy was drawn with the aircraft industry, where competition was suspended and different firms were coerced to tackle intercontinental or short-haul airliners. Official specifications were issued much as they had been for fighting aircraft in the late war. The strategy had its successes, such as the Airspeed Ambassador and the

Vickers Viscount, but also its expensive and spectacular failures, such as the Princess flying boat and the Bristol Brabazon.

Sir John Black of the Standard Motor Company was one of the few motor industry heads who were persuaded, and committed himself to a car self-consciously styled to look like a 1942 American Plymouth. Appropriately bearing the name of Britain's last battleship, the Standard Vanguard might have been better had Black not overruled his designers.

They wanted to lengthen the 94in wheelbase, against its 164in overall, which would have given the car better proportions. Instead it appeared foreshortened and stubby, and although it proved robust and serviceable enough, it was unsuitable for many markets overseas. After selling tolerably well at first (185,000 in the first five years - but anything on wheels was selling well), sales waned as soon as market forces took over.

Standard was burdened with the car for seven years. All that was left was the simple wet-liner, four-cylinder 2-litre engine, which thrived long after the car had gone. The day of the world car never arrived, and in some desperation Standard introduced an Eight and a Ten in 1953. By then 'wasteful proliferation' was in full swing and the motor industry

cheerfully put the crisis years and government direction, for the time being at any rate, behind it.

Rover took note of Standard's moves, and underwent a number of reactions to the predicament in which it found itself. The first was the time-honoured one of planning an economy model, but in the light of the experience of the Eight of 1919 and the Scarab of 1929, Rover was older and wiser.

This time it would not try a popular economy model. There was no point in competing with Ford or Austin, well established with production lines and substantial factories geared to making cars in large numbers. Rover argued instead that there would be a market for a small and economical luxury car in due course, and set one of its engineers, Gordon Bashford, to design it.

It was a measured reaction to the privations of the late 1940s. 'Down-

Loading up for the export drive but damage in transit was a problem. Soft bags cushion the effects of the sling, but this Rover has already lost lens and reflector from its pass-lamp. (left)

Rover 16 1946/47. (top right)

sizing' had not yet entered the motoring lexicon, yet here was Rover adjusting to circumstances, with a solution that would be adopted again in years to come. Spencer Wilks's intuition was not at fault. Rover would once again enter the market for compact-sized cars with the luxury characteristics of larger cars, but not just yet.

The engineer behind Rover throughout the 1930s and 1940s, Maurice Wilks. (above)

Signal of progress, semaphore arms trade-named 'Trafficators' soon gave way to flashing indicators. (right)

The choice of Bashford, who had been with Rover since 1931, was critical. He played relatively minor roles - he drew up the front section of the important 1937 cars - until 1945, when he returned to the Rover design and engineering staff from reworking the Rolls-Royce Merlin into a tank engine. He had just turned 30, but displayed such capacity that the day after the war in Europe ended, he became responsible for a good deal of the development of post-war vehicle design under Maurice Wilks and later Spen King.

Bashford worked in a small outpost of the design office, a wooden hut at Chesworth Grange near Kenilworth. He still reported to the head of design and the assistant chief engineer, but he was able to exercise his own initiative.

He drew up the M-Type 6hp, which never went into production, and developed Rover's first in-house independent front suspension. Rover had not exploited independent springing because channel section chassis frames, like those of most manufacturers, were not stiff enough. The M-type, designed from the start as a monocoque, followed more advanced practice where the suspension was expected to do the springing, not the chassis frame.

The M-type had an innovative spot-welded structure, made up of small

aluminium pressings, showing Rover was well aware of such voguish ideas in 1945. Bashford learned a great deal from his connection with the aircraft industry (he had been seconded to Rolls-Royce with the gas turbine team), and had worked on small racing car projects, such as the scarcely remembered Djinn.

Just as his contemporary, Alec Issigonis, showed with his Lightweight Special, so Bashford persuaded Maurice Wilks of the virtues of aircraft-style lightweight aluminium structures. He developed them into the racing tub form of construction, later used to good effect for both single-seat and two-seater racing cars.

"Steel may have been in short supply, but there was a lot of aluminium about after the war. The aircraft industry used it and it was cheap," Bashford said. By the 1950s aluminium was used quite extensively, albeit sometimes only experimentally, in cars built in relatively small numbers.

Wilks and Bashford explored small cars, such as the Fiat 500 and the innovative aluminium French Dyna Panhard, and drew up a structure with a 77in wheelbase (3in shorter than a Mini) and aluminium castings bracing the scuttle. It was 13ft 4in long (6in shorter than a Rover 200). The engine was a compact 699cc

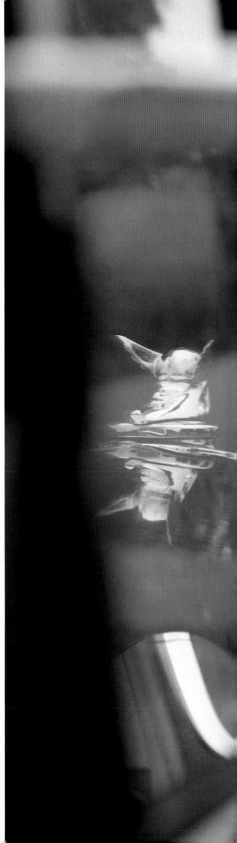

four-cylinder, based on the inlet over exhaust (ioe) valve unit undergoing development for Rover's main large cars, with a power of 28bhp.

Coil spring and wishbone independent front suspension, and a live rear axle located by a Panhard rod with coil springs, promised good behaviour on the road and a two-

The 75 was available as a six-light saloon (right) or sportier four-light. (above)

door body of engagingly modern shape was evolved by Harry Loker. An open coupé was drawn up as well and three prototypes were built.

All the ingenuity came to naught and by 1947 the project had been cancelled. Once the flat rate car tax came in, and steel supply eased as defence contracts were run down, Wilks decided that small cars - even luxury small cars - held little attraction, and instead he set Bashford to work revising the Girling 'pyramidal' suspension for the P3.

Rover first tried independent front suspension (ifs) in the 1930s, and catalogued the 1935 Speed 14 with a coil spring system. Developed by Girling, it was similar to the one used by Lanchester in the 1930s, with a lever-arm shock absorber forming the top link and long radius arms underneath.

Pyramidal was a name coined to emphasise the system's careful triangulation, with the inclined top links and joints pivoting on the rearmost pick-up point on the chassis, so that there was no twist in the rubber-bushed bearings.

Unfortunately it turned out to be such a burly composition that there was precious little saving in unsprung weight. The low-rate coil springs provided a smooth ride on

European roads, but some P3s exported to territories with dirt roads and long-wave undulations bottomed out to such an extent that 150 customers had to be given their money back, and the cars were withdrawn from the market.

Wilks nevertheless became convinced that an era of long-travel springing was at hand. Customers were demanding more ride comfort - they had grown accustomed to American cars, which had developed softer springing in the 1940s - and Rovers intended for export would need to conform.

But as he found with the M-Type, soft springing demanded a stiff chassis, so he boxed in the channel-section framework of the P3 chassis. A new stiffer chassis for the P3 had been on the stocks in 1939 with a 110.5in wheelbase. This was somewhere between the old Rover Ten and Twelve, but shorter than the Fourteen or Sixteen. The track was wider at the back, slightly narrower at the front with the independent layout, and the all-steel, as opposed to ash-framed, body was a wider version of the one introduced in 1937. The call for a smoother ride brought an innovation at the rear of the chassis. The old underslung frame provided more space inside by banishing the chassis members underneath, but it placed a serious limitation on spring movement.

Bashford could provide no more with an underslung chassis, but chassis members climbing over the back axle would have meant reverting to a back seat of cramped 1931 size.

His ingenious solution was to do away altogether with the frame at the rear. The chassis members ended ahead of the rear wheels and the ends of the semi-elliptic springs, gaitered to keep in their oil and run quietly and reliably, hung on a crossmember mounted in the rear of the body. The Girling arrangement at the front was amended, so that the wheels remained vertical from full bump to rebound, an unusual asset in independent systems of the 1940s.

Rover's continued dedication to quiet running resulted in rubber bushes in the suspension linkage. Modern maintenance-free bearings allowed the old chassis lubrication system to be abandoned at last. Maurice Wilks, conservative to the end, was reluctant to give up mechanical brakes, so the P3 compromised with hydraulics at the front and rod-operated at the rear.

Hydro-mechanical brakes were not unusual in the 1940s, but they were an uneasy concession, and the P3's were not as good as the mechanical system they replaced. The change to hydraulics only became necessary at

all because rods and cables could not be adapted to independent front suspension. The new arrangement was least good at slow speeds. Lighter steering was contrived, with a Burman recirculating ball which used a variable ratio for reducing the effort at parking speeds.

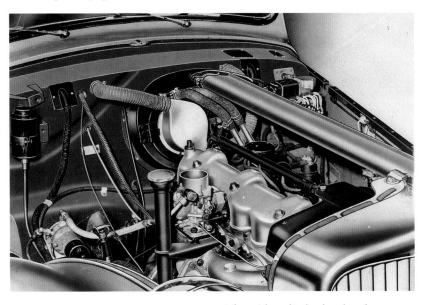

Overhead inlet and side exhaust valve (ioe) engine under the bonnet of the new Rover 75. (above)

The body was wider and fatter, the bonnet short, and the engine was set well back in the frame, yet the lines of the car were unmistakeable. It was fifteen years since the Hastings Coupé had emerged yet the symbolism and proportions were identical.

The wide cylinder head and crankcase of the ioe engine meant widening the engine compartment of the P3, and Harry Loker, who had been responsible for Rover styling since the late 1930s, was engaged to redesign the body. He tried a number of treatments to the grille and headlights, in an effort to meet what the management saw as the fashions of the day. There was no question of changing the rest of the car. That would have been an unwarranted expense in a post-war market in which facelifts were not essential prerequisites to sales, so the doors, boot and roofline remained unchanged.

Like Austin with the A40, Hillman with the Minx, and even pillars of the establishment such as the Armstrong-Siddeley Hurricane, a full-width front seemed indispensable.

The results were not encouraging. Sinking the headlamps into the wings, chiselling out a cliff-like facade, and smoothing off the wings into an amorphous mass did nothing for the car's good proportions and completely destroyed its dignity. Proposals came and went, models were built and viewed with distate. Even quite good designs were not pursued with much enthusiasm. Rover was convinced that its chief market would remain in Britain, and was determined that its traditional doctor, solicitor and business customers would be served first.

A proposed interim model was abandoned. Production of the 1937-1947 P2 was now well-established in Solihull, and the only way forward was to start work on a radically new car.

The P2 developed into the P3, without major changes to its silhouette beyond widening and refining, mostly through a certain amount of indecision over the appearance. By the time of its introduction however, time for the old body shape was running out. Development of the P4 was well under way, and the P3 became a commercial test-bed for the new engine, transmission and suspension.

Reduced to little more than an interim model, the final phase of the P3 only lasted a year and a half. Pressure from the planners goaded Rover into a certain amount of standardisation, announcing in the P3 sales catalogue that the company had '*decided to produce one chassis model with a choice of four or six cylinder engines*'. It was pure semantics and exactly what the company had been doing before. It may have seemed to the central planners that Rover was following the example of the Standard Motor Company, and been persuaded by the wisdom of a one-model policy.

Rover's second reaction to the post-war crisis was the Land Rover. The result was a success of incalculable importance to Rover and to the motor industry in the Midlands.

In a third reaction to the new circumstances, Rover took the essentially practical step of making the cars acceptable to overseas customers. For the first time production had to be engineered for both righthand and lefthand drive.

A four-cylinder prototype of Jack Swaine's projected 1930s V-6 gave such good results that Maurice Wilks decided to adopt the combustion chamber shape for post-war Rovers. Export markets were looking for sophistication, and Wilks was well aware of precedents such as BMW, which had been notably successful in the 1930s with an engine in which a cross-pushrod arrangement converted it from sidevalves to overhead valves.

Rolls-Royce had adopted the F-head, as the ioe arrangement was called early in the century, forsaken it, then returned to it in 1938 as successive developments of the 20/25 and 25/30 demanded ever larger valves. The amount of metal between the valve seats became so small, and the castings so fragile, that water cooling space was problematical. Rolls-Royce rejected overhead camshafts on the grounds of noise from drive-shafts or chains, so the only way of accommodating large valves was to put the inlets in the head and the exhausts at the side.

Sceptical engineers thought the oddly shaped combustion chambers would constrain the high compression ratios adopted during the 1930s to take advantage of modern fuels. Yet Rolls-Royce was able to go from 6.4:1 to 8.0:1 during the period it employed ioe engines between 1947 and 1959.

The experimental ioe engine, built for the stillborn M-Type in 1945, gave encouraging results showing Wilks that a production engine was practical. It also had the advantage in the context of the late 1940s of having a combustion chamber with excellent turbulence which happily burnt the weak mixtures of the current low-grade fuel.

His view might have been revised had the M-Type gone ahead, because a change in the taxation system swept away the old RAC Treasury rating and introduced a flat rate irrespective of engine size. The RAC formula took only the cylinder bore into account, so designers retaliated by making engines with small bores and long strokes to place cars in a lower taxation class than they perhaps deserved.

Engines with long strokes and small bores meant small valves and cramped combustion spaces, but after the introduction of the flat rate designers were able to contemplate well-proportioned cylinder dimensions, bigger valves and improved efficiency.

The new legislation was framed to give designers freedom to create engines for world markets. Unfortunately, it came too late for Rover to reverse its ioe policy, conceived under the old order. Still, the refinement argument held good,

and Rover secured an exemplary power unit.

The new 1,595cc four-cylinder would have been 11.98hp, and the 2,103cc six 15.81hp under the old Treasury system. Rover could not shake off the old habit of calling cars by horsepower, however, and the 12 became the 60 because it produced 60bhp, and the 16 was the 75 which was a small deception since it only developed 72bhp.

The valves were driven off a single camshaft in the side of the cylinder block, the exhaust valves working through one set of rockers at an angle of 55 degrees from the vertical. The inlets were worked from the same camshaft, through two lots of rockers and pushrods. The face of the cylinder block was inclined at 20 degrees in relation to the cylinder axis, so the inlet valves were vertical, and the compression ratio of 7.2:1 was satisfactory for Pool petrol of about 75 octane RM.

There were two versions of the engine for the P3. The Rover 60 had the four-cylinder, and the 75 the six-cylinder version. Cylinder bore and stroke dimensions of 69.5mm x 105mm were identical in both cases, giving capacities of 1,595cc and 2,103cc. The four had a three-bearing and the six a five-bearing crankshaft, and respective power outputs were 60bhp and 72bhp.

The scene was set for the next phase of Rover passenger car development, the radical P4. But before it could start, the legacy of the war-time jet engine would engage the attention of some of the best and brightest brains in British industry.

Tidy stowage for the hood in the 1948 drophead coupé, a revived version of the pre-war model. Dashboard includes freewheel control to left of instruments. (above)

CHAPTER VI

Rotary Rovers

Power unit for the future?
(above)

The individuals who played key roles in developing Rover's later post-war technology under Maurice Wilks were cousins Spencer King and Peter Wilks. Nephews of Spencer and Maurice Wilks, neither ever needed to rely on family connections to make their way.

Peter Wilks died prematurely after a brilliant engineering career, and Spen King went on to become engineering director of BL Cars, but his best work took place when he had the freedom of action his brilliance deserved at Rover.

King was an apprentice at war-time Rolls-Royce, becoming involved in gas turbines following Rover's withdrawal from aircraft engines. He described Rolls-Royce as a generous university. *"Rolls-Royce was in the process of learning a lot about the engine itself. It was fundamentally new, no one had a text book, and there was a lot of bright people wrapped up in the new subject."*

Rover decided belatedly that there might be a future for gas turbines in cars, and in 1945 set up a project unit with Frank Bell and King, based at Solihull. The result was the first gas turbine engined car, JET 1, which set records for the flying kilometre at Jabbeke in Belgium at almost 152mph and produced a succession of prototypes that nearly brought a gas turbine car into production in the 1960s.

In a 1974 interview with the author Graham Robson, King was asked if there was a point at which it became obvious that the gas turbine would not be viable in a car.

"No, I don't think there was. But trying to do something that was only dubiously possible was a bit wearing. One of our cars, T4, was a serious proposition but we were unable to make it good enough in terms of cost and fuel consumption to be competitive. But the project wasn't costing a great deal of money and we produced useful engines anyway - for the Vulcan and Argosy (the last Coventry-built aircraft) for instance."

The aircraft engines were auxiliary power units (APUs), and Rover-Leyland gas turbines were also used

The gas turbine made a comeback in the 1990s as a generator for hybrid cars. In the Rover T4 it drove the front wheels through reduction gearing. (right)

for British Rail's Advanced Passenger Train (APT) programme in the 1970s. The APT was designed originally with a Rolls-Royce Dart engine, but the prototype APT-E had four 300shp (224kw) automotive gas turbines identical to those used experimentally in trucks, with a fifth doing much the same APU job, supplying the power for non-driving systems and air-conditioning.

Pre-heating the air, by means of such heat exchangers, repressed the engine's demand for large quantities of fuel. Early experimental cars ran at between 4 and 6mpg of kerosene. The other drawbacks included the high temperatures and pressures it ran at which, in aircraft applications, could be met by using special expensive materials. A car or truck turbine, Bell and King reasoned, should be made of simpler stuff.

Their other problem was a practical one. The power turbine was relatively slow to run up to 25,000rpm (the compressor turbine was doing 40,000rpm) and the effect on initial start-up and acceleration was profound.

Rover's first gas turbine project was a tiny 25bhp unit, too small for any practical use, but it led on to a larger engine developing 230bhp at 26,000rpm. This was installed at the rear of a standard P4 chassis, equipped with a version of the abandoned convertible with three-abreast seating, and was demonstrated in March 1950 as JET 1, the world's first practical gas turbine car.

In 1952 it was brought out again, lightened and taken to a stretch of uncompleted motorway at Jabbeke in Belgium, and set speed records at almost 152mph. Spen King and Peter Wilks set up a series of records including the standing kilometre at

Linking the present with the future

Most of the essential chassis features of the Rover Seventy-five, including suspension and steering, have shown their worth by being used unchanged in the 150 m.p.h. gas-turbine car.

The ROVER Seventy Five
ONE OF BRITAIN'S FINE CARS

THE ROVER COMPANY LIMITED, SOLIHULL, BIRMINGHAM AND DEVONSHIRE HOUSE, LONDON.

Rover constantly sought to relate gas turbine research to its road car programme (above). JET 1 lost its cyclops central headlight in later life.

Rover BRM at the Le Mans test weekend, April 1964. (right)

The advantage of the gas turbine was continuous power by means of a centrifugal air compressor, a combustion chamber where burning fuel heated the air, and a vaned wheel spun by the hot air. It was rather like a blowlamp turning a swiftly rotating fan, and worked best when the waste heat was used to warm up the incoming air.

132.596kph (82.391mph). Rover felt bold enough to set up Rover Gas Turbines Ltd to develop engines for industrial and automotive applications. JET 1 earned Rover a second Dewar Trophy before it was retired to the Science Museum.

Two years later, a 120bhp turbine was installed in the engine bay of a P4 75, with the exhaust gases ducted to the rear, but it proved impractical and was quickly scrapped. Its successor, T2A, was again rear-engined with a huge exhaust gas duct blowing skywards from the tail.

The T3, the third experimental model, was shown at the 1956 Earls Court motor show. Designed from the start as a complete gas turbine car, it featured four-wheel drive, a rear-mounted twin shaft 110bhp engine, and a two-door, glass reinforced-plastic body.

Designed almost as a private project by King, with Bashford as his draughtsman because the development department was, as so often in Rover's crowded history, preoccupied with new passenger cars, T3 proved to be a turning point. It demonstrated how resourceful its two designers were, and set out a number of features later found on production Rovers, including the De Dion axle and inboard disc brakes of the 2000. Once a heat exchanger was fitted, the T3's fuel consumption improved to between 10 and 12mpg. It was a brilliant conception, but it represented the apogee of gas turbine car development.

King's final fling was to design the P6, with an engine bay large enough to accommodate a gas turbine engine, should a technical breakthrough occur during its lifetime. In practical terms, the T4 gas turbine saloon revealed in 1961 was based on the P6 prototype structure, with the 140bhp twin-shaft engine at the front driving the front wheels. It would reach 60mph in eight seconds, and the fuel consumption was 20mpg, but it took ten seconds to reach idling speed from a cold start.

King told Graham Robson: "*T4 was very serious, but we weren't able to make it competitive in terms of cost or fuel consumption.*"

A great deal of Rover 2000 detailing was complete by the time T4 was built, although it predated the announcement of the production car by fully two years. The seat patterns, the door trims, the rounded open facia with the wide parcel shelf were all in place. Even the switchgear was all to the 2000's pattern with different shapes for every purpose. The specialist chrome trim, most of the body pressings, and the general proportions all carried heavy hints of how the 2000 would ultimately appear.

The interior had the extra instrumentation appropriate to a

The comprehensive solution. Rear-engined, four-wheel driven, the T3 was designed as a gas turbine car from the start. (far left)

Dewar Trophy (left) awarded to Rover three times.

Maurice Wilks on left shows T3 to Donald Campbell. (above)

at Le Mans in 1963 and 1965, but so far as passenger cars were concerned it proved uncompetitive with the piston engine. The high cost of materials, and the special techniques necessary to make components with them, proved insurmountable obstacles throughout the 1950s and 1960s. Even the development of ceramic heat exchangers, to recover heat energy lost to the exhaust, was not enough to achieve acceptable fuel economy. A gas turbine car needed twice the fuel tank capacity of a piston-engined car for the same range.

Following the first oil crisis of 1973, and the growing demands of emission control regulations, interest in gas turbines revived slightly. Progress in materials technology, including the vital role of ceramics, encouraged developments in the 1980s. Reputable engineers once again looked at gas turbines, in specialised steady speed applications in trucks and hybrid turbo-electric vehicles, to enter service before the end of the century.

T4 1961 switchgear was from still secret Rover 2000. Console included large pressure gauge, instruments for elapsed engine life, oil temperature and pressure, turbine temperatures up to 300°C. (above)

JET 1 with project engineer Frank Bell on left and Maurice Wilks. (right)

prototype. The two pods in front of the driver revealed how David Bache saw the 2000 at that stage of development: they were like full-sized mock-ups of his sketches of early interior treatments. The driver's dials contained a speedometer and a gauge for the jet temperature - the passenger watched an ammeter, oil pressure and a fuel gauge.

Rover's dalliance with the gas turbine engine was not over until the 1960s. William Martin-Hurst revived interest in it with the Rover-BRM that raced

CHAPTER VII

Cyclops modern Odyssey

The P3 Rover 60 and 75 did little more than buy time. Rivals were forging ahead with cars which, although often little more than warmed over designs of the 1930s, looked as though they might have been intended to last into the 1950s. Bristol, Daimler and the Humber Hawk gained full-width bodies, and by 1948 both Jaguar and Armstrong-Siddeley were well into their post-war programmes.

It was characteristic of Rover to do the engineering first and worry about the cosmetics afterwards. The biggest difference between the appearance of the P3 and that of its predecessor was 2in extra width. When the P4 came in the autumn of 1949 it marked a major change of strategy. It was seldom Rover's habit to be radical. Extreme measures were almost unknown in a company that preferred evolution to redesign. It was prudent to develop cars gradually rather than undergo the risky business of bringing out something totally new.

In the case of the P4, much of the engineering was already in place in the

P3. Only the body was completely fresh. It was also startling, in a way never seen on a Rover before and seldom if ever again.

In 1946 Maurice Wilks was searching for inspiration for a new body shape suitable for the markets of the world. That summer, in America, he was sure he had found the answer. Studebaker, the oldest car manufacturer in the United States, stole a march on its competitors with the announcement of the striking looking 2.8-litre Champion and 3.7-litre Commander. Wilks was convinced they were going to set a styling vogue, and quickly arranged for two to be bought in conditions of great secrecy and brought to Solihull.

Studebaker was determined to break new ground after the war. Defence contracts left little time for staff stylists to work on cars, but one consultant was not restrained by making armaments.

Raymond Loewy Associates had a new car ready for Studebaker to put into production, while its rivals were still

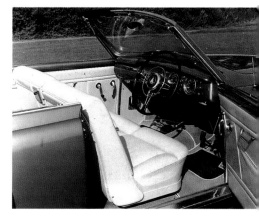

Interior of 1953 P4 convertible made by Pininfarina. A prototype never put into production. (above)

Sales brochures glamorised 1950s look, jazzed-up P4 like Vauxhall Cresta and Ford Zodiac. Too baroque, like the wedding-cake building behind. (left)

making thinly disguised versions of what they had been building in 1942.

Loewy was a clever publicist, whose appliqué design theories had already changed the shape of American railway locomotives and long-distance buses. It hardly mattered that Pennsylvania Railroad express trains had no need of streamlining; their sleek shapes became part of the romance of rail travel in the 1930s.

The Studebakers that Loewy and Virgil Exner designed created a sensation. They had short bonnets and long tails. Critics complained they could not tell the front from the back; there were no separate wings, the curves and creases in the body mouldings only hinted at such traditional features.

What Loewy had done was write a new lexicon of car styling. The front-back confusion missed the point of the design, for he effectively invented the three-box configuration - engine, passenger compartment and boot - that became the classic shape of the modern automobile. Until the advent of the Studebaker, the wings and the engine compartment and the passenger compartment were identifiable component parts of a car.

Now they were integrated with smooth curves or body-joins, no longer features in their own right, and after the best part of half a century the motor car had become all of a piece.

In the Studebaker the old functions were scarcely discernible. Loewy's wrap-round rear window led to badinage about glasshouses, but it established the flash-sided full-width car in the public eye, and rendered everything else obsolete. The three-box design became the convention, and although the three-piece rear window wrapping into the body sides was not widely copied at first, the Studebaker idiom set the pattern for an entire generation.

Wilks wanted it to set the pattern for the new Rover 75, but he was unable to overcome his own inhibitions, to say nothing of those of his colleagues. He could not bring himself to reproduce the Studebaker's forward-leaning prow or jet intake snout. Rovers somehow had to retain their customary dignity. He needed help in assessing the new shape, and for the first time the designer and Harry Loker had clay models made to help them. One of the Studebakers had its body stripped down and put on a P4 chassis, which it fitted almost perfectly. It became known within the works as the Roverbaker and was used for several years before being rebuilt as a Studebaker.

Prototype P4s were made, with sculpted sides and a smoothed-off three-box shape, clearly following Loewy's pattern. The tail with raised centre was pure Loewy, but the wrap-round window had to wait until 1954

before attaining the original's broad sweep.

Wilks expected the dramatic style of the P4 to open up export markets for Rover, and while it did in some instances, some of the traditional clientele were outraged. It took Rover's steadfast commitment to good quality, and high standards of refinement and silence, to bring them round.

Those who remained faithful to Rover did not, as a rule, do so because the styling was an unqualified success. Something about the proportions was never quite right. The turn-out at the bottom of the doors was a distraction and the small windows looked mean. The mouldings of the wings and bonnet produced too many small radius curves; Loewy's rendering was homogeneous, Rover's was a collection of disparate shapes.

Determined to keep the customary three-lamp system at the front, the P4 75 had a central pass-lamp in the middle of a decorative grille. It earned the enduring nickname of Cyclops, after the one-eyed Cyclopes, the storm deities of Greek mythology. It was a mistake. The pass-lamp and the chrome trim blocked off cooling air and were renounced in 1952.

With the introduction of the P4, Rover felt it had overtaken its rivals, with a true post-war design. Others, such as

Publicity shots for
Cyclops. Westminster
model points her bellows
camera up Victoria Street.
(left)

Rear-hinged back door
demanded glance
rearwards for traffic
before opening.
(above right)

Standard with its Vanguard, had committed themselves to a style that had been a passing fad in 1942.

The P4 retained some capricious features. Its doors closed on the central pillar. Apart altogether from occupants colliding with one another getting in or out, it produced rear-hinged back doors, condemned on safety grounds even in 1950. The sloping boot floor was a constant source of anguish. The bodies were made by Pressed Steel at Cowley, and up till 1963 the bonnet, doors and bootlid were aluminium. The paintwork was done with much obsessive attention to quality and refinement.

Inaugurated in the P3, the six-cylinder ioe engine now projected well ahead of the front wheels' centreline, shifting the occupants forward within the wheelbase. This meant that the rear seat was now clear of the graceful upsweep of the chassis over the back axle. The result put 56 per cent of the car's weight on the front wheels leading, in the euphemistic world to which *The Motor* was still committed in 1950 to, '*under, rather than over-steer... the car follows a true course on the straight..*'.

In fact it tended to follow a straight course on corners too, and it was only with the advent of the four-cylinder

Rover 60 in 1954 that the proportion of weight on the front fell below 53 per cent.

Yet if the exterior was radical, the chassis structure would have been recognised in some respects by Owen Clegg. Conservative engineers at Rover did not yet trust monocoques, so a chassis stiff enough to accommodate independent springing had to be drawn up, strong enough to carry the striking-looking new body. The side members were formed into a sturdy box section by closing off the open side of the channel sections, and the suspension was changed, with telescopic dampers and longer bottom

links at the front. There was a Panhard rod at the rear to keep the car steady on corners.

The P4 frame was so rigid that six insulated rubber mounts each side held the body in place, without it playing a structural role. The forward engine mounting enabled the chassis to reach the rearmost spring hangers without cramping the rear seat, because the occupants were now placed firmly within the wheelbase. This arrangement not only gave them a better ride (at the expense of rear seat legroom), but enabled a curvy Studebaker luggage boot to go into the flowing tail. It was not a large boot, but it was neatly trimmed and bigger than any Rover hitherto.

The engine was changed from the P3 with an aluminium cylinder head, designed by Jack Swaine, lightening it by 30lb (13.6kg). The cylinder bores were chromium-plated, another reassuring feature shared with contemporary Rolls-Royces. Rover had no more luck with it than Rolls-Royce, which equipped the Silver Wraith with chrome bores in an effort to stretch engine life to 100,000 miles between major overhauls.

By 1950 some Rolls-Royces were reaching 90,000 miles without any trouble, but others suffered bore wear by 40,000, as the .0015in thick chromium wore through. Idling in traffic was held to blame. If the engine

never warmed up properly and the oil failed to circulate, chromium cylinders did little good, so Rolls-Royce changed to short liners with 30 per cent chromed instead.

Rover also reverted to non-chromed bores in due course, but persisted with painstaking production techniques, including rigorous engine testing. Every engine went on one of the Tyseley plant's 45 water brake test benches for five hours. They were run electrically and balanced, which could take up to an hour, with weights added to the clutch or the crankshaft damper to try to make them as free from vibrations as possible. At the peak of its activity in the late 1950s, Tyseley, which had been acquired for the Rover Eight in the 1920s, had more than 3,500 people working a five-day week.

Body finishing was no less obsessive. New bodies had a rubber sound-proofing solution underneath and on the bulkheads. Five coats of primer were applied and rubbed down, followed by two coats of enamel sprayed wet on wet, and baked. Extra paint was applied round the doors, bonnet and bootlid because they had to cope with the effects of slamming. Every car was rubbed down after it was finished, then cleaned and wax polished before it was delivered.

When two-colour paintwork came in, customers could choose whether to have the darker shade on the top or on

the bottom. Final assembly took place at Solihull, where chassis frames made by John Thompson Motor Pressings were machined.

Rover factories were scattered over a wide area. Springfield manufactured experimental and development items and reconditioned machine tools; Ryland Road supplied steering and suspension parts; Percy Road provided finished axles and transmission units; while gearboxes were sent to the engine factory at Tyseley.

The interior of the new 75 was restrained. The only Studebaker feature was a half horn ring on the steering wheel, and the facia was plain and flat with small rectangular instruments in a metal frame hinged to give access to the wiring. The timber was solid West African walnut, polished to bring out the grain, so no two cars were ever quite alike. The curved corner fillets were made of aluminium, so veneer matching the real woodwork had to be applied to cover them up. The two locker lids were also of polished walnut, with cabinet-maker's concealed hinges. Rover had its own trim shop to make the frames of the adjustable front seats.

The bulkhead was felt-lined, and the body undersealed, a popular treatment to try to fend off rust. The transmission housing was undersealed and sound proofed. Felt headlining was reluctantly abandoned in the

By the 1960s the P4 was tidied up. The central headlight had gone. (left)

Two-tone paintwork spread as a fashion fad found few friends among conservative customers. (above)

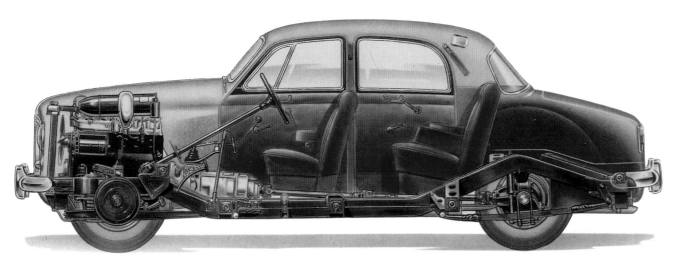

1950s, and replaced with washable plastic only when Rover was convinced it would be as quiet.

The celebrated rubber-lined wooden tool tray was hand-made in the Rover works, and the heater controls were made by Smiths to Rover's design, so that they worked smoothly. Rover specified how the chrome-plated radiator grilles had to be made, with contrasting slats of polished, rustproof alloy. The window surrounds were walnut, the carpets a comfortable pile, the seats leather, and plain like the P3. They came with the quaint period option of felt or plastic covers, which kept the leather fresh for subsequent owners.

Contemporary rivals such as Mercedes-Benz were less munificent. The mid-range 190 still generally came with plastic seats, rubber covering on the floor, and a brown plastic facia with curvy lines to make it look like wood. Expensive French and Italian rivals had cream-coloured plastic

switchgear and steering wheels. Their engineering was often of a high standard, but the minor controls looked cheap and vulgar compared with Rover's.

Among the 75's options were a screenwash kit, badge bar, extra-loud windtone horns, footrests in the back and floor mats. It could, in short, be furnished like a contemporary Rolls-Royce.

Rover's fastidious methods were described by William Boddy, editor of *Motor Sport*, in 1958. '*Five water brakes are used for endurance engine testing, with tests of up to 700 hours or even to destruction, made at every change in specification material.*'

Gearboxes were tested for five minutes in drive and over-run on a large electric motor. Boddy was impressed by Rover thoroughness in measuring the strength of front suspension coil springs, then pairing them so that a slightly stronger one was fitted on the

driver's side to ensure a level ride height when they settled.

'*Rubber insulation is used liberally in the Rover chassis. The front suspension radius arms are set in rubber, rubber rings are fitted under the coil-springs, and rubber insulates the back springs. The complete front suspension assembly is first lined-up correctly on a special jig and the rear leaf-springs are liberally greased before gaiters are fitted.*'

Rover's attention to detail included attaching the fuel lines to the top of the chassis frame and making the steering idler arm from an alloy casting, with precision-cut splines.

'*Rover has a rigid inspection system for raw materials and outside-supplied components with a ratio of inspectors to operatives in the region of 20%. The firm has its own laboratory, and takes test-pieces from castings before they are machined. Transfer cylinder-block machining is used for Land Rover engines but not for the car engines.*'

Ingredients of Rover 75. Inlet over exhaust engine, chassis frame upswept over back axle, steady bearing to reduce propellor shaft vibrations, shepherd's crook handbrake, cranked gear lever, drum brakes, ifs and half-elliptic springs at rear. (above)

Not for the last time American road testers applied superlatives to a Rover. The Rolls-Royce analogy was never solicited but invariably welcome. (right)

Every connecting rod is inspected for bore size and ovality on an air gauge, to half-a-thousandth of an inch. Starter-ring teeth are hardened by electrically heating each ring to 850 deg.C. and then quenching it in water, an operation carried out automatically in a special cabinet.

'Gudgeon pins are graded after machining to 1/10 of a thousandth of an inch, camshafts are hardened both in the furnace and by the new gas carburising process, and components such as rocker-shafts are crack-tested. Pistons and connecting rods are checked and graded in special pressurised rooms kept at an even temperature. Sets of six pistons all of identical weight are made up, five grades being recognised, within two drums, and every connecting-rod is balanced and the gudgeon-pin bore checked to within half-a-thousandth of an inch. Every valve seat is individually ground-in, tested by blue-ing, then tested again with petrol under compressed air.

'After assembly the oil-gallery of each engine undergoes a pressure check. In these and many other ways is the reliability of the Rover engine ensured.'

The only major design revision found necessary for the P3/P4 ioe engine, during its fifteen-year life, came for the revised 75 of 1955 and the high-performance Rover 90. The cylinder bore centres were altered to accommodate an increase in size to

2,230cc and 2,630cc. More generous water passages were also created by the change, which was incorporated into the 1,997cc Rover 60 engine.

Since the P4 engine was such a long way from the back axle, the propellor shaft was unusually extended. A thin shaft might have spun, vibrating like a skipping rope, and a thick one would have been heavy. Rover's solution was to divide the shaft in the middle with a steadying centre bearing. No expense was spared to sustain the reputation for quietness and refinement. Otherwise the clutch and gearbox were much as they had been in the old, upright and traditional-looking 75.

The new 75 was higher-geared, but kept the freewheel in a housing aft of the gearbox, making it necessary in Rover's view to have synchromesh only on third and top. The Rover freewheel, by now unique, was also a touch bizarre by the 1950s. It still enabled the driver to change gear without touching the clutch, or it could be locked out of action for drivers who preferred a conventional if somewhat leisurely transmission. Changing into second demanded double declutching to achieve a totally smooth shift.

The freewheel could be brought into operation to help fuel consumption, but without any engine overrun effect this meant heavier use of the brakes, not unimportant with drum brakes

that lost a good deal of efficiency when hot. The freewheel did impose a novel discipline on a driver intent on smoothness. Anticipating traffic in good time to slow gracefully resulted in progress like that of a good chauffeur.

It was not until 1953 that synchromesh was extended to second gear. Laycock de Normanville overdrive was available on the 90 from 1955, on the 60 and 75 the year following, and became standard on the 105, 80 and 110.

Besides the 'Roverbaker' styling, the 75 made two further concessions to fad and fashion. It had a steering column gearshift and a bench front seat. The gearshift was designed with great skill by Frank Shaw, without any cables and with the gear positions for top and third at arm's length from the wheel. The seat was supposed to take three abreast.

Both were follies. Round about 1946 British car designers, in a collective leave-taking of their senses, decided that in order to export to America it was necessary to have steering column shifts and bench front seats.

It hardly mattered that cars were not wide enough to take three people side by side, and Americans hardly ever seemed to bother to try (except in moving pictures). It was the conventional wisdom and Rover played along with the fantasy.

It was never satisfactory, and the Rover distributor in Birmingham even offered a conversion devised by Spen King and Peter Wilks for owners who disliked it. Customer resistance to the thing eventually wrought a change on the introduction of new models in 1954. Once Rover had seen the error of its ways and Shaw's work was put to one side, a new central gearshift was brought in. It was a triumph of ingenuity, achieved by careful workmanship and good detail engineering. A swan-necked remote-control lever served for the remainder of the P4's life, and worked rather better than it looked as though it had a right to.

An adjustable bracket, and a long cranked spring-steel handle, allowed the possibility of three-abreast seating by means of a mounting ring. It could be moved bodily sideways to bring the lever close to the driver. The change was not fast. It had a deliberate, precise movement, quite in keeping with the relaxing nature of the car.

The P4's handbrake was also somewhat idiosyncratic and worked rather better than it looked. On the right and ahead of the driver, it was barely within reach on early cars, so for 1950 an extension was added, which lent it an unusual shepherd's crook shape. It had a strong and well-made ratchet and worked with a reassuringly positive movement.

Rover 90. Last Rover with a separate chassis, the P4 had best part of 50 years' engineering expertise behind it.
(left)

Sectioned exhibit for the Earls Court motor show reveals overhead inlet valves and independent front suspension.
(right)

There were second thoughts on that, too, in due course. A pull-up lever on the right was brought in for 1954, but by popular demand the shepherd's crook was reinstated in 1956, and it endured for the remainder of the life of the car.

Rover switchgear and controls had the feel of quality machines about them, long before design psychologists concluded they were a positive help to sales. The Wilks brothers were prescient in identifying tactile qualities, such as switches that clicked, handles that felt secure, locks that did not grate, and doors that excluded wind noise and traffic sounds. The courtesy light switches were beautifully made by Lucas to Rover's design.

The four-cylinder 60 was discontinued on the introduction of the new 75 for 1950, Rover somewhat belatedly falling into line with 1945 doctrine and adopting a one-model policy.

The mid-1950s were full of innovation. In France the Citroën DS 19 created as much of a stir as its 'Traction' forebear had in 1934. In Germany Mercedes-Benz was back on its feet, winning great motor races and establishing a technical ascendancy that made it a formidable rival in the markets of the world.

Freed at last from shortages and restrictions, buyers were once again buying. Ford and Vauxhall introduced

cars that lay close to Rover in size and specification if not in quietness and refinement. In Britain petrol was plentiful until the Suez crisis of 1956, and a £212 million road programme announced by the Minister of Transport, John Boyd-Carpenter, included proposals for the country's first motorways.

The scene was set for a new, fast Rover, and the six-cylinder 2.6-litre 90 at last acquired Loewy's wrap-round, three-piece rear window, which the conservative Maurice Wilks had shunned. David Bache joined as body designer in 1953 and began work on a larger boot, ironically robbing the car of its last real Loewy feature, the distinctive humped boot lid.

The 90 had a substantive 93bhp, but its low compression ratio was a sure sign

that there was more to come. The single SU carburettor had integral water passages and expensive manifolding, while the twin SU layout of the 105 underwent still more modification.

The P4 90 abandoned the freewheel, introduced overdrive and went through to the start of the next decade and another new car, the P5. Meanwhile, there was yet another new model, the P4 105R in 1957 with Roverdrive, a short-lived two-speed semi-automatic not notable for its speed of operation.

In the autumn of 1956 came the twin carburettor high compression version of the 90, giving 108bhp and becoming the 105R (for Roverdrive automatic) and 105S (for Synchromesh manual transmission). Author Michael

Frostick had an alternative explanation of the titles. The S, he claimed, was for the more sporting, the R for the more retired.

The manual 105 of 1957 was lively and robust, with a top speed of nearly 100mph and a fuel consumption of just under 20mpg, although *Motor Sport* magazine did not much like the brakes which '*worked spendidly for a time and then let the pedal descend to the floor on the next application*'. It was a problem which it hoped '*...has presumably been overcome on the many 105S Rovers still in service*'.

In the mid-1950s it seemed that an automatic revolution might be on the way. In America two-pedal cars had been the custom for years, and by the way of these things it seemed likely that the practice would spread to Europe.

The 105R unveiled at Earls Court in 1956 was intended to produce much the same effect as a torque converter and epicyclic gearbox such as the American Hydramatic. It had fewer components, it absorbed less power, and it was cheaper. The torque converter, an automatic clutch filled with oil, acted like a turbine to multiply the engine's pull by 2.5 times. It smoothed the flow of power at the expense of greatly increased fuel consumption. Rover's home-grown torque converter used oil from the engine sump, a servo-operated clutch,

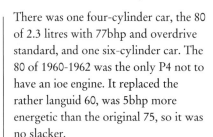

and instead of the epicyclic gearbox it had a two-speed Laycock de Normanville overdrive.

It might have been satisfactory for big, powerful V-8s, but it proved scarcely adequate for a relatively small six-cylinder, with not much power to spare. It still absorbed a good deal of energy and the 105R's acceleration turned out to be not much better than the 60's. Accordingly an emergency low gear was provided, with a simple synchromesh gearbox and vacuum-operated friction clutch. For most driving the torque converter and the two-speed gearbox worked well enough. Hill starts or steep ascents meant falling back on the low gear.

Within eighteen months it was dropped. Demands for fuel economy in the wake of Suez were blamed, but it was a complicated system that never found much favour with drivers. Once the P5 3 Litre was available, with a better sort of automatic, it was gratefully abandoned.

A number of experimental P4s were tried, including one with a 3-litre engine and Borg-Warner automatic transmission. But by the late 1950s, the valve train was nearing the limits of its performance, and the proposal was rejected. Instead of being developed further, the P4 took on the role of a second division Rover. The P5 3 Litre became the flagship, so for 1960 the P4 range was tidied up.

Mark IX saloon in the hotel car park was a reminder of the constant threat Jaguar posed to Rover.

(left)

There was one four-cylinder car, the 80 of 2.3 litres with 77bhp and overdrive standard, and one six-cylinder car. The 80 of 1960-1962 was the only P4 not to have an ioe engine. It replaced the rather languid 60, was 5bhp more energetic than the original 75, so it was no slacker.

The engine was a rather bleak-sounding variant of the Land Rover 3-bearing diesel, and early models suffered from timing-chain clatter. On the credit side, four-cylinder P4s always handled better, the lighter engine imposing less understeer. The 100 of the same period had a 2,625cc short-stroke version of the 3-litre 7-bearing roller cam-follower engine. In 1963 the six-cylinder was standardised in the 95 and the 110, and the aluminium body panels were replaced with steel.

The last in the line, the 110, gained much the same sort of approval when *The Motor* tested it in 1963 as it had on its introduction as the 75 in 1949. '*The 75 is a car which will be found equally satisfying to the pernickety requirements of the sedate connoisseur and to the more exacting requirements of the man who habitually drives fast and has a keen appreciation of handling qualities.*'

The Motor's assumption that Rover drivers would be male probably raised no eyebrows. The testers achieved a top speed of 83.5mph and a fuel

consumption on Pool petrol of 27.8mpg. Acceleration to 60mph took 21.6sec. Smoothness, refinement, and '*.. a degree of mechanical quietness which despite some wind noise makes conversation pleasant even at maximum speed*' were commended. The modern full-width coachwork and frontal treatment were portrayed as '*distinctive and functionally sound,*' even if it '*offended some conservative tastes*'.

By 1963 *The Motor* regarded the 110 as '*a faster version of a formal car*'. Top speed was up to 100mph, acceleration to 60mph improved to 15.9sec, but the fuel consumption was down to 18.4mpg. After fourteen years, the design was described as traditional rather than simply conventional, and other cars had caught up with the interior layout of switches and levers.

'*The layout of the facia and controls looks a little haphazard as a result of all the alterations that have been made to it over the years.*'

There was criticism of the visibility from the driving seat, past windscreen pillars grown unfashionably thick, and the only corner of the car visible to the driver was the offside front. The boot was out of sight which made reversing difficult.

By the standards of the 1960s there were some areas for concern. While mechanical noise was successfully subdued by careful attention to engine balance, and most sounds were eliminated at their source, wind noise had become an issue. It was not a question of the car's unaerodynamic shape, so much as less-than-perfect seals round the swivelling quarter-light

panes in the front windows. Other cars, such as Jaguars, were proving a match for Rovers in more ways than speed and handling.

Heavy steering at parking speeds was a further reason for the decline in the P4's sales as the 1960s drew on. The car rolled on corners more than its

contemporaries, and customers were growing fussier over details such as the slope on the boot floor. Luggage slid towards the rear so that slots had to be provided for securing straps.

By the 1960s, the 110 looked dated. The Loewy derived styling did not stand the test of time well, despite afterthoughts such as a recessed grille and more prominent headlights. Rover's aim was to provide it with a family resemblance to the P5 3 Litre introduced in 1958. The fuss over the styling was probably, in the end, scarcely justified. Maurice Wilks, for all his professed unawareness of style, had a keener eye for shape and proportion than he was given credit for. Yet the car never gained much acclaim for its shape and tended to make the press and the customers hesitant.

The Autocar praised it somewhat faintly in 1956, claiming doubtfully: '*The car has something about it which is difficult to describe. It tends to make the driver try to drive better than he usually does, a feeling which has occurred with only one or two other cars; they were equally out of the top drawer.*' What the magazine's road test staff was saying in effect was: '*As keen drivers we find it hard to be enthusiastic about the Rover; we know we ought to like it and it is difficult to pin down what is wrong with it, because so many people seem to relish it.*'

Spring sunshine in the mountains above Lac Leman, Rover demonstration car pauses on the way back from the 1958 Geneva motor show.
(above)

Early P4s had rectangular instruments and steering column gearshift. Second thoughts included Radiomobile, swan-necked gearshift, round instruments, padded roll on the facia, and a badge instead of the freewheel control left of heater.
(left)

First Land Rovers were strongly agricultural.
(right)

It was difficult for the generally enthusiastic drivers of *The Autocar* staff to allow that, once again, Rover had matched its product with uncanny precision to a niche in the market.

The mood of the buyer was captured; Rover somehow identified its customers and built them the right merchandise. The Wilks philosophy, laid down in 1930, held good in 1950, and before the 1960s were under way it scored again.

To William Boddy, the most convincing evidence about Rover quality came with the final factory road test of new cars: '*This is carried out on Rover's own road circuit and every car and Land Rover is submitted to it. Two independent drivers test each car, although routine tests cover about two laps in the hands of the first driver and three laps by the other, a total of 12-15 miles. If defects are found anything up to a week may elapse before a car is passed out. Such items as tyres out of balance, noisy clock and loose wheel nuts are checked, besides the obvious sources of trouble. Only this extremely thorough testing of components, engines and completed cars satisfies those responsible for maintaining the Rover reputation. Even then every car is put on a 'bump machine' in a sound-proofed bay so that squeaks and rattles, if any, can be located and rectified.*'

A total of 130,342 P4 Rovers were

made between 1949 and 1964, of which only 15,161 had four-cylinder engines. The model spanned the period from the end of the traditional classic erect Rover with a chassis and a tall radiator and free-standing headlamps, to the P6, one of the most innovative Rovers ever and a turning point in the design of the modern car.

Boddy's endorsement was unequivocal. '*It is pleasing to find Britain still building fine motor cars to the highest standards -Rover obviously considers durability and silence as important as performance. Under the circumstances, the fully-equipped Rover 90 at £1,499 17s, inclusive of purchase tax, is not so expensive as it might seem. We have frequently cited it as offering excellent value-for-money. After having seen the conscientious care that goes into every facet of Rover manufacture and testing, we readily endorse this opinion.*'

CHAPTER VIII

P5 and Fond du Lac, Wisconsin

Among Rover's principal engineers throughout the critical post-war years were Gordon Bashford, who retired in 1981 as BL Technology's chief engineer for advanced vehicles, and Spen King, the archetypal motor industry boffin. King thought of nothing but cars, and the problems associated with their design, often to the despair of those who worked with him. Routine office work held little charm for King, but his gift for fundamental thought and research brought about some of the most original Rover cars ever.

Bashford was mainly responsible for putting the design work of Rover's output from the 1940s to the 1970s into practice. His work included the Land Rover, the experimental M-Type, the 1947 revisions to the P3, and the pivotal P4.

The masterpieces of the 1960s, the P6, the mid-engined sports car the BS, and the Range Rover, were still to come. These were the brilliant creations of a team under the technical director Peter Wilks, with Spen King and David Bache. But in the 1950s there was a gap in Rover's model range which Bashford, as deputy chief engineer, played a critical role in filling.

Only Jaguar was making a success of the market above that of P4 with its 3.4-litre Mark VII. Armstrong-Siddeley was in decline, despite a few fresh new models, such as the 234 and 236. Alvis was moribund, although it still had a trick or two to play with the Graber-bodied 3 Litre. Daimler was in contention with the Conquest, but none could approach Jaguar's prices.

Perhaps neither could Rover, but it could give the customer something Jaguar could not - not yet at any rate - and that was a touch of class. Jaguars were still a little outré, a trifle racy. Rover could provide a car that would represent another milestone - the P5. Introduced in 1958 as the Rover 3 Litre, it departed from the traditional pattern of chassis frame and body, which had served since Edmund Lewis's imaginative ventures of 1904. Integral structures were not altogether new. They had been produced widely in Britain since the 1930s; they were light, cheap, stiff and easy to make.

HM the Queen's 3.5-litre P5 at Windsor.
(right)

Stylised version of the Viking ship used on P5 Coupés.
(left)

Draught excluders on the side windows distinguish this pre-1961 3 Litre. (above)

Engine and gearbox were mounted on a sub-frame fixed to the body at six places. (right)

The chief drawback of dispensing with the chassis, and making a complete one-piece car by spot-welding dozens of steel pressings, was noise. Building a car like a steel drum could make it sound like one, and designers found the reverberations difficult to eradicate. Felt wadding did not always work because the echoes through the steel were often too strong.

The rationale behind the one-piece, or monocoque, construction was undeniable however, and Rover knew the problem would have to be solved. Others might fudge the issue, put up with some noise, for the sake of getting

a car's weight down or speeding production.

Since 1930 Rover had made its name through silence and refinement and it was not going to relinquish it lightly. The idea of unitary construction had been toyed with for the P4, and rejected because of noise. The car was now the epitome of good manners, its quietness was an industry benchmark. The solution to the dilemma, posed by a proposal in 1953 for a car smaller than the P4 to be made in quite large numbers, looked like a compromise.

The form of construction that evolved was known as base-unit, in which a skeletal frame was built up and the outer body structure and the mechanical units hung on to it afterwards. It had the advantages of being easy to silence and strong. It was not entirely novel; Edmund Lewis had been thinking along base-unit lines in 1904 with the Rover Eight, and Olaf Poppe had made a similar proposal in the 1930s.

Its disadvantage was principally the expense of pioneering. The volume car idea was abandoned, because Rover still did not have the resources to compete with Ford and the British Motor Corporation. BMC was formed in 1952 with the amalgamation of Austin and Nuffield (Morris, Wolseley, MG and Riley). The mighty Ford motor company was shaking off its pre war mantle of cheap and

cheerful, with strikingly styled Consuls and Zephyrs. Between them they accounted for well over half the cars sold in Britain. Rover, by contrast, was making 40,000 cars a year in the middle 1950s, two-thirds of which were Land Rovers. So instead of setting out to design a car smaller than the P4 to be made in large numbers, Bashford was told to start work on a larger car to be made in small numbers. The base-unit idea was, for the moment, set aside and Rover's first conventional fully integrated body-chassis monocoque took shape.

Some mechanical parts were not altogether new. Jack Swaine restarted work on his 1930s V-6 project in 1950, once again with the inlet-over-exhaust valve layout and sloping cylinder head. Engines of various sizes were drawn up, a 3-litre, then a 2-litre, followed by another 3-litre. The carburettors were mounted on the outside of the Vee and the exhaust was routed out through the middle.

It was not a success. Breathing was the main problem, prototypes were never able to reach much over 4,000 rpm, and power output was disappointing. Instead the six cylinders of the P4's familiar ioe engine were bored out to 78.8mm, to produce an engine with a capacity of 2,995cc, delivering 115bhp at 4250rpm.

It was not an easy task within the dimensions of the existing cylinder

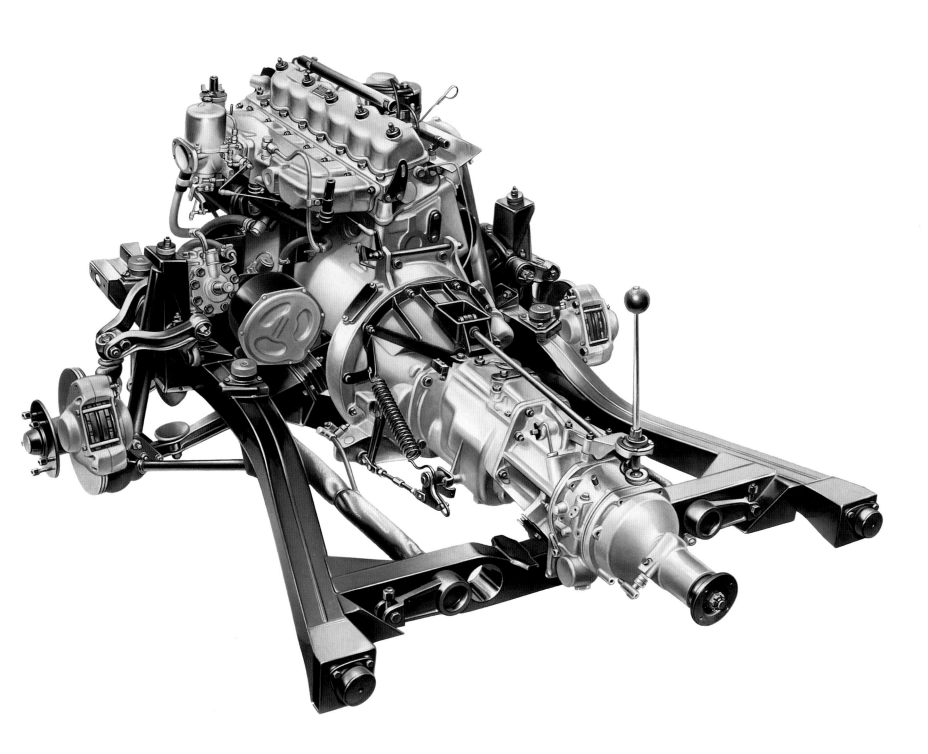

block. One possibility was to bore out the cylinders from the 73.025mm of the Rover 90 engine to 77.8mm and fit the same pistons as the 60, but the walls would have been thin. Further complication arose when Maurice Wilks decided, in the interests of quietness and refinement, that the crankshaft would have seven main bearings in line with current practice. It was already current practice at Jaguar, where the XK engine was setting another industry benchmark for power and smoothness.

Wilks was determined to have a stiff crankcase, and water between the cylinders, so the cylinder centres were moved apart. It made the 3 Litre engine bigger, but the increase was modest.

The cylinder head followed the 90 closely, except for some improvements to the valve gear to save wear, and the compression ratio was raised to take advantage of the new high-octane petrol becoming available. Oil companies had long known that adding tetraethyl lead suppressed detonation and provided a short-cut to the widespread use of 100 octane fuel. Blending agents were developed during the war for aviation fuel, and the motor industry soon designed suitable engines, which promised more power without heavy fuel consumption. It seemed that an era of highly efficient engines was at hand, although the modest power of the

3 Litre made the first production cars rather languid.

There was plenty of development to come, but with 115bhp at 4,500rpm, the enlarged engine was not much more powerful than the 108bhp twin-carburettor Rover 105. It took a leisurely 16 seconds to reach 60mph, two seconds slower than the ponderous Armstrong-Siddeley Star Sapphire or a Jaguar Mark VII automatic.

A Coupé, with the roofline lowered by 2.5in and the rear seats moved forward and more clearly divided into two, was developed concurrently although not introduced until 1962. The intention, like that of the speed model Rovers of the 1930s, was to meet the demands of customers not content with the performance of the saloon versions.

Its engine should have been a development of the 110's which, at 123bhp, was the most powerful P4. The cylinder head was recast with a separate manifold, and a combustion chamber was developed by Harry Weslake, founder of the engine research consultancy.

It was not ready in time for the launch, and in due course went into the Mark 2 versions of both cars in 1963. Economy versions of the 3 Litre using a 2-litre four-cylinder, or a 2.6-litre six-cylinder, were not sold in Britain once it became clear how torpid they

Mock-up P5 erected outside factory in 1955. Details changed included radiator and windscreen sunshade. (top left)

Low roofline Coupé. (bottom left)

Coupé colour schemes differed from saloon in 1965 advertisement. (right)

were going to be. Experiments with multi-carburettor layouts were put in hand, but none produced much improvement, except at the cost of intake noise or loss of flexibility. The car went on sale to a mixed reception from a market accustomed to refinement, but expecting, in view of the competition, a livelier car.

Jaguar was making its mark, not only among fast car enthusiasts. It was gaining ground in refinement, and Rover had no choice but to meet the competition. It could not afford to appear dull or slow. Leisurely performance had, for the time being at any rate, gone by the board.

Styling the 3 Litre demanded a subtler approach than the Studebaker copying of the 1940s. Among Rover's responses to the dubious reception accorded the Cyclops 75 was to commission Pininfarina, one of Italy's leading designers, to devise a two-door drophead body. A number of elective styles were evolved, including a two-door P4 made by Tickford in 1950-51. Two drophead prototypes were made along the lines subsequently adopted for JET 1, the gas turbine car. There was also a two-door fixed-head coupé, but none went into production.

The drophead coupé created by Pininfarina late in 1952 followed the lines of his contemporary Lancias and Alfa Romeos. It was followed by the

handsome fixed-head coupé shown at Earls Court in 1953, and this was the car from which the P5 3 Litre evolved. The traditional tall slatted radiator grille, characteristic of Rovers for more than twenty years until the P4, was broadened and reshaped.

Pininfarina probably saved the grille for Rovers in later years. It had been

abandoned for the early P4 but was brought back in 1952. It returned for the P5, was nearly lost again in the P6, disappeared altogether in the SD1 and had to be rescued from oblivion yet again in 1991. The shape and style built into the 1953 prototype was kept on ice until the 3 Litre was ready, even though the exquisite proportions and fine detailing achieved by the Italians

proved difficult to put into production. The press and public response to the Pininfarina coupé was eager. Another was built by Mulliner as a production study, but results were discouraging. It would have been costly to make, and the sales department was not convinced there were sufficient customers for such a sleek and 'haute couture' production.

Rover's other response to the cool reception given the P4 was the appointment, under Maurice Wilks, of 26-year-old David Bache to supervise what was still called the styling of future Rovers.

'Design' is a more appropriate term, and Bache left his mark on an entire generation of Rovers, which gained

distinction in almost every area that he influenced. Bache studied at Birmingham University and College of Art, while a student apprentice at Austin, which he joined in 1948. He came to Rover, fresh from six years at Austin, and immediately joined Gordon Bashford to work on the broad outline of a new big saloon using the 2,994cc engine.

Bashford found himself committed to the monocoque body for reasons of economy, weight, and style - a chassis made a car tall. Bache shaped it up, followed some of the precepts of the Pininfarina car, and the design crystallised as one of the most elegant and dignified Rovers.

Bache's interior for the 3 Litre was a masterpiece. It continued Rover's traditional pattern, with a wide panel of solid West African walnut and a deep parcels shelf, and a separate instrument binnacle ahead of the driver. It was a triumph of well-placed switchgear and clear controls set in a calm, well-furnished environment.

In one sense it was the last in a line of Rovers that used solid wood, if not for structural function, then at least for good practical reasons. The glovebox lid and the picnic tray were best in wood; it was something more than cosmetic. Pile carpets, deeply pleated leather, and rolls of padded soft cushioning round the parcels shelf -

a safety feature - rounded off a style that was fast passing into history.

Engineering conservatism had one last hurrah in the design of the 3 Litre. The body was monocoque in the true sense, but the engine, transmission and front suspension were carried in a small mini-chassis of their own. Rover was still apprehensive about noise vibration and harshness. Its reputation for Rolls-Royce-like silence was now so precious that a sub-frame, with six rubber mountings to carry the engine and front suspension, was deemed necessary.

The caution came about through criticism of monocoque hulls used on contemporary cars that was not entirely misplaced. Bashford's team tried everything they knew to make the roomy 3 Litre quiet. Tyre noise was suppressed, engine silencing improved, sound-damping materials were added, yet when it did appear, despite all efforts, it was not as quiet as the P4. Resonance, seemingly inseparable from a monocoque hull, emerged as the principal culprit. There was apparently still a good deal to learn about the art and science of making a 'one-piece' car.

Some notable advances were made at the expense of conformity, which sat a little uneasily on Rover shoulders. Rover solutions had consistently been the right ones rather than the most expedient. It seemed like expediency to

offer manual transmission with a Laycock de Normanville overdrive, as on many British middle-class saloons of the time. It smacked of standardisation. It was not exactly a betrayal, but Rover using the same proprietary unit as lesser makes was still not quite the thing.

The automatic transmission was not a Rover design either. The one tried in the P4 105R in 1956 and found wanting was discarded, and in 1958 the 3 Litre acquired a Borg-Warner automatic, as the 105R was phased out.

Borg-Warner transmissions became almost universal on Austins, Vanden Plas Princesses and Wolseleys, Armstrong-Siddeleys and Jaguars.

The 3 Litre's front suspension was something of a return to convention with orthodox wishbones, sprung by means of laminated torsion bars. The use of torsion bar springing was unusual enough, with the 3 Litre's made up of leaves to save the expense and complication of machining the usual steel bar. There was a certain amount of head-shaking even at this apparent short-cut, but the system worked well enough and conferred a satisfactory high-speed ride.

The suspension could be caught out by long-wave bumps, which set the rear axle hopping, and some uneven

French-market P5 had 2.6-litre engine, whitewall tyres and explanatory grille badge.
(left)

Six-cylinder 3 Litre inlet over exhaust engine filled bonnet space.
(right)

surfaces made the car pitch, which the dampers found difficult to control. There was also a good deal of body roll on slow corners.

The live rear axle, too, was less than satisfactory. Drivers who decided to take part in a traffic light grand prix were more than likely to suffer the embarrassment of axle tramp. Letting out the clutch swiftly could result in the axle hopping, in a succession of crashing thumps, against the rubber bump stops before settling down to drive the car forwards.

As in the contemporary P4, the freewheel was abandoned. Leisurely gearchanges could no longer be tolerated, there was little virtue left in freewheeling as an aid to economy or silence, and the higher speeds and greater weight of cars resulted in a strain on the brakes in export markets unfamiliar with such subtleties.

The P4's swan-necked gearshift did not carry over well to the 3 Litre, nor did the drum brakes, which were replaced by front-wheel discs after one season. The non-power-assisted steering was heavy at slow speeds, making parking a laborious affair, and it was not as precise as a Jaguar's. The 3 Litre also suffered from tyre squeal, which could be an embarrassment in town. Even the Avon HM crossply tyres that Rover had, for the most part, fitted as standard equipment since the war protested a good deal.

In an effort to meet critics of the heavy steering, the Hydrosteer variable-ratio system was offered as an option in 1961. It was less than entirely satisfactory, and the 3 Litre's steering still felt lifeless, and inappropriately weighted.

It was difficult to avoid the conclusion that the P5 failed to obtain the test and development attention it deserved. It certainly had a difficult example to follow; P4 owners were unswerving in their loyalty, and perhaps mistook the 3 Litre's aim as being the Jaguar market, which it was not. It was an alternative for drivers who did not want the speed of a Jaguar, who valued comfort and silence and roominess, and who did not want to stoop to get in and out of a car.

Yet it was considerations of speed and style that lay behind the improvements that it underwent in the autumn of 1962. There was no escaping the influence Jaguar created in the market for luxury cars. The Mark VII was large and imposing, and although deliberately marketed with a sporting image reinforced by racing successes at Le Mans, both it and in 1955 the new 2.4 litre selling at extremely competitive prices, made inroads on Rover's traditional market.

The 9ft 2.5in wheelbase and 15ft 6.5in length of the 3 Litre corresponded to the Mark VII's 10ft and 16ft 4.5in. The Rover cost £1,715 and the Jaguar

Characteristic sumptuous leather upholstery.
(left)

Toolset hand-made in the Rover factory fitted in drawer below facia. No rattles from sorbo rubber moulding.
(left)

£1,903. Fuel consumption was comparable at around 19 to 21mpg with the Rover having a slight edge; the Jaguar had more headroom in the back, but less in front and the greater length gave extra legroom.

The principal difference was in acceleration and top speed. The Jaguar was a genuine 100mph car, while the Rover could barely manage 90mph in direct top, or 95mph with a good run-up in overdrive. More power for the P5, the management concluded, would not go amiss.

Jack Swaine's engine initiatives were not leading to success. The most likely prospect was that they would come right in the end, but the end was not yet in sight when William Martin-Hurst visited Mercury Marine's experimental department at Fond du Lac, Wisconsin.

Martin-Hurst came from the aircraft industry in 1960 to join Rover as executive director for production, and progressed swiftly. By 1962 he was managing director, and called on Carl Kiekhaefer, head of Mercury, to discuss production of a marine version of the Land Rover engine for fishing boats in the Far East. On the shop floor Martin-Hurst spotted a compact aluminium V-8 being made ready for one of Mercury's boats.

It was a Buick, which had been taken out of production after only three

Carefully detailed David Bache interiors. Instrument binnacle had switchgear aligned with steering wheel rim. (right)

years in the Buick Special, Pontiac Tempest and Oldsmobile F-85 Cutlass. General Motors abandoned it after managing to make thin-walled iron castings for V-8 blocks, which were almost as light in weight and a good deal cheaper, than the elegant die-cast aluminium unit lying on Mercury Marine's floor.

Martin-Hurst not only knew of Swaine's difficulties with the 3 Litre, he was also growing concerned about the future of programmes taking shape for the 1960s, such as the P6 and P7. The sales department had misgivings

about a large four-cylinder engine in the proposed P6 - it was worried about smoothness and quietness again - and the six-cylinder was turning out to be too long to fit the space available in a mid-range car. A five-cylinder was being tried but seemed to be presenting as many difficulties as it solved. The alternative of different base-units for the four and the six cylinder renderings of the P6 was not attractive economically, so when Martin-Hurst caught sight of the little redundant aluminium Buick, he was immediately interested. It was only half an inch longer than the four-cylinder engine

Historic meeting at
Mercury Marine between
William Martin-Hurst (on
the right) and Carl
Kiekhaefer led to Rover's
adoption of the
Buick V-8 engine.
(above)

for the projected P6, and left space to spare in the wide engine bay of both it and the current, slow P5.

GM made three-quarters of a million examples of the 3.5-litre V-8 before forsaking it, together with a 5-litre, large-bore cast-iron unit of similar design. Martin-Hurst learned that it weighed only 12lb more than the P6 four-cylinder, and it would be a great deal lighter and 8in shorter than the envisaged six-cylinder.

The handling of the prototype P6 was already causing concern with the rather large and heavy six. Martin-Hurst realised that an engine like this

would solve many of the problems besetting the 3 Litre as well as the P6.

Kiekhaefer agreed to air-freight the engine to England while Martin-Hurst hastened to the New York motor show to make contact with General Motors. His mission was to negotiate the terms of a licence to make it. The question of whether it could be made to Rover standards of silence and refinement could wait.

The V-8 engine was still something of a novelty in Europe, except for the old side-valve Ford long out of production. At about the time of Martin-Hurst's visit to the United States, BMW had almost abandoned the 2.6- and 3.2-litre aluminium V-8 it introduced in 1954. The European market, it concluded, had no use for a V-8. Nearly all the V-8 engined cars in the 1960s, such as Jensen, Facel-Vega and Bristol, had American engines and two exceptions, in the eyes of a Rover chief executive, were critical.

One was Rolls-Royce. The 6.2-litre 90-degree V-8 introduced for the Silver Cloud II in 1959 had an aluminium cylinder block and hydraulic tappets. Rolls-Royce would have liked to use thin-walled cast iron for the cylinder block, but discovered that the foundry techniques were unavailable outside America, so made it in aluminium.

To GM this cast-iron route was open, and with money to spare, the

aluminium engine could be forsaken.

The other European V-8 that was important to Martin-Hurst was made by Daimler. Jaguar took over the British Daimler company, founded in 1896 and long since separated from its German forebear, from BSA in 1960. It inherited two V-8 engines, one an old rather leaden 4.6-litre in the surprisingly spirited Majestic Major, the other a much younger 2,548cc unit designed by Edward Turner of the Triumph motorcycle company.

It was drawn up for the short-lived Daimler SP250 sports car and after the Jaguar takeover was squeezed into a Mark 2 Jaguar body as the Daimler 2.5 Litre. It was a smoother engine than Jaguar's own short-stroke 2.4-litre, the handling was better since the engine weighed over a hundredweight less, and it was more powerful at 140bhp against 120bhp. Since Daimler was more associated with luxury than Jaguar, it sold as an upmarket version of the 2.4, with the new Borg Warner Model 35 automatic transmission, at a price close to the Rover 3 Litre. The small V-8 Daimler did 110mph and reached 60mph in 13.5sec. Turner's engine would have needed a large investment to produce in large quantities, but the car continued until August 1969 as the Daimler V-8 250, and represented a challenge Martin-Hurst could scarcely ignore.

America was the spiritual home of the

V-8. The US buyer had taken them to his heart in the 1940s, mostly at around 5.0 litres, and they suited the size and style of American cars. GM turned to a smaller-capacity V-8 for the compacts of the 1950s, equipping it with hydraulic self-adjusting tappets to make it as quiet as a big engine.

So with one of Rover's role models, Rolls-Royce, in production with a V-8, and one of its rivals, Jaguar, with another, Martin-Hurst began negotiations with General Motors. He met Buick executive vice-president Ed Rollert, who told him that GM had been unable to make the pistons work directly in aluminium bores, so after a great deal of research and development went to cast-in cylinder liners instead.

GM used a Heron-style flat cylinder head with the combustion chamber in a shaped hollow in the piston. The two divisions using the engine had not liked this, because it enforced the use of high-octane fuel, which American motorists seemed reluctant to pay for. Accordingly each division had designed its own heads, although the results were much the same, except that the Oldsmobile had more studs holding it down. The Americans could scarcely believe Rover was serious at first and it was two years before agreement was reached. Rover gained the manufacturing licence in 1965, together with all the planning sheets and drawings, and machinery to make it. The engines' service records and 39

that remained in stock were handed over so that Rover could start development work straight away.

It demanded a certain amount of political skill on Martin-Hurst's part to get the idea through. Peter Wilks was less than enthusiastic, but once an engine was put into a prototype P6, he embraced it happily. The main changes needed from the start were a new exhaust manifold, and downdraught SU carburettors in place of the multi-choke Rochester.

Rover's commitment to refined engineering suffered no lapse with the American engine. Included in the agreement with GM was an American engineer, Joe Turley, who was within a year or two of retirement and no longer worked on new projects. He had forty years' experience of GM, and knew enough about the history of the 215 cubic inch V-8 to brief Rover on its history and the reasons behind many of its features.

Turley's advice was invaluable in further shortening the time it took to get the engine into production, incorporating many of the modifications and improvements GM had built into it. The main difference was changing the cylinder blocks from gravity die castings to sand castings. A foundry was specially built by the Birmingham Aluminium Casting company to make them, and press in the centrifugally cast cylinder liners.

Rover took over Alvis in 1965, which provided a well-equipped machine shop making aircraft engines. Machining of the V-8 was carried out there, and assembly was at Acocks Green, the former shadow factory where the Meteor tank version of the Rolls-Royce Merlin engine was made.

Other changes included raising the compression ratio to a formidable 10:1. British motorists were expected to obey the injunction to fill with high-octane petrol.

Once installed in a 3 Litre, the engine fulfilled all Martin-Hurst's hopes. It was 200lb lighter than the old straight six ioe unit, removing some of the burden off the front wheels and

One of Rover's motives in taking on V-8 came from rival Daimler which used an inherited 2.5-litre V-8 to good effect in a Jaguar Mark 2 body. (below)

reducing the car's chronic understeer. Early 3 Litre cars had 115bhp, the Mark II 129bhp, and the Mark III 134bhp. A 1964 3 Litre Coupé took nearly 18sec to reach 60mph, had a top speed of 102mph, and managed only 15-17mpg. The 3.5 P5B (for Buick) with the V-8 and 185bhp did 110mph and reached 60mph in about 10.5sec with negligible fuel consumption penalty.

The V-8 P5 was only ever sold with automatic transmission. The old manual gearbox, essentially similar to the one fitted to Rovers in the 1930s, was no longer up to the job and was pensioned off. It was perhaps pensioned off too late; criticism of Rover ponderousness generally began with the clumsiness of the gearshift and the absence, until rather late in the day, of synchromesh on second gear. Some rivals were fitting it to first gear before Rover allowed it on second.

The freewheel probably concealed some of its shortcomings, but it was certainly not up to the job of dealing with the V-8's power, around four times what had been in its designers' minds around 1934.

In many ways there was still an affinity between a Rover and a Rolls-Royce. The bodies were both made by Pressed Steel at Cowley, and the richness of the interiors was not unalike. It took a careful eye to detect the Rover's plastic headlining. The

Rover's woodwork had a solid appearance - the Rolls-Royce's was polished with jeweller's rouge. The Rover's leather had all of a Rolls-Royce's hand-stitched appearance, although in both cases the hands were helped by sewing machines.

Rover had a Borg Warner automatic; Rolls-Royce chose a Hydramatic. Rover's sub-frames were mounted in rubber; Rolls-Royce's in a cushion of compressed steel gauze. Rover's V-8 came from America; Rolls-Royce's was home-grown.

The difference of course was numbers: Rolls-Royce's handful of cars against Rover's best year for the 3 Litre (1962) when 7,445 were made. In all, nearly 70,000 P5s were turned out between 1959 and 1973 against 130,300 P4s, paving the way for the most numerous of all, the P6.

Deeply curved screen and Rostyle wheels identify P5B of 1967. (right)

Rover prices were just breaking the £2,000 barrier in 1968. (below) Prime Minister Harold Wilson was an early customer.

Rover announce the incredibly Smooth new 160 bhp 3·5 litre V8. With apologies.

CHAPTER IX

Best 4x4 By Far

The Land Rover was either a triumph of design or an accident of expediency. The facts were never in dispute. The prototype was copied from a Jeep. It was introduced at the Amsterdam motor show in April 1948, as something of a stop-gap to see Rover through a difficult market and a national steel shortage.

Rover owed its survival as a manufacturer to this astonishing vehicle, which saw service not only on the quiet farms for which it was intended, but in every desert, jungle, swamp, mountain and trouble spot throughout the civilised and uncivilised world.

The Land Rover was expected to see farmers and small businesses through the austere aftermath of the war. Its development occupied barely a year, it was in production by July 1948, there was a pre-production run of 48 vehicles and Maurice and Spencer Wilks expected to make about fifty or so a week for a year or two. Within twelve months 8,000 were sold. Within two years this had

reached 24,000, Rover was soon making 1,000 a week, earning more than £5 million a year overseas.

Sales spiralled. By 1959 the total was over 250,000, by 1966 half a million, by the 1990s it was racing towards two million and production looked certain to continue well into the 21st century. Many of the humble pioneer examples of the 1940s survived, cherished by collectors, as revered as any sports car of the Vintage era.

Yet when Harold Hastings, the Midlands editor of *The Motor*, was shown the first prototype, he was dubious about its commercial prospects. '*It was a vehicle intended to bash over fields in far-flung parts of the empire on unmetalled tracks. So why should it be built with the same care as a Rover 60? Surely something more agricultural would be better and cheaper.*'

It did have a Rover 60 luxury car engine, but only to make things easier for its creators. The stop-gap nature of the design and the production process made it necessary

Ancestor. The prototype Willys-Overland quarter-ton General Purpose (GP) 'Jeep', delivered to the United States Army on 11 November 1940. (above)

Uphill work for a Land Rover. (left)

to use existing components. It seemed pointless to introduce a new engine for a vehicle of which only a few hundred might be sold in the space of two or three years.

It was one occasion when the Wilkses' prescience seemed to desert them. They never took into account the success that would attend the Land Rover. The aim was to keep the price below £450 and the hood, the spare wheel carrier, the starting handle, and even the doors and passenger seat were intended to be optional extras. In the event they were all included in the price. The prototype Land Rover had the driving seat in the middle, ostensibly because a farmer might want to use it instead of a tractor. Early publicity pictures showed one pulling a plough.

According to Gordon Bashford: '*We built the prototype with Jeep axles and with a central steering wheel. The idea was that it was going to be a farmer's vehicle and if the farmer was going to have a plough behind it, he'd want to be in the position of the horse.*'

A more credible explanation for the central seat lay in an endeavour to persuade the authorities that it was an agricultural vehicle, and thus not subject to British purchase tax. The body was made in aluminium to frustrate the Ministry of Supply

bureaucracy, which controlled the company's steel allocation.

The Autocar called it '*A practical road and cross country vehicle built to high standards*', which it remained. It kept its appearance and its character, and although subject to so much development that after some years hardly any component parts of the Mark 1 remained, it was still recognisably a Land Rover.

An anomaly of the shortages of 1947 was that although steel was in short supply, aluminium was relatively plentiful. So as soon as Maurice and Spencer Wilks identified an area of the market into which they could drive, a vehicle with plenty of aluminium in it looked like a good idea. Their preference was for a new small car, and work began on the 699cc M-Type with an aluminium chassis. When it became clear that it could not be made in sufficient numbers to fill the factory space Rover had acquired during the war, it was abandoned.

The Wilkses were in a quandary. They faced a government demand that they export or suffer a reduction in their steel allocation. Unfortunately, the only cars in production were pre-war designs, and there were many pitfalls in tackling overseas markets with unsuitable merchandise. It would be some time before a new model was ready, so a radical alternative that could be brought to production quickly was sought.

Prototype Land Rover had one central seat (top left)

Production model had three seats, doors, aluminium body. Spare wheel on bonnet increased carrying room (top right)

Bombed out of its Helen Street plant in 1940, Rover moved its war production into a vast factory at Solihull, and as large areas were cleared for peace-time production it became too big for making cars. Rover had official licence to make no more than 1,100 cars because there was not enough steel to make more.

Something else had to be found to fill the vacant space, and once the M-Type proved a non-starter the Wilkses were forced to look instead at a small all-purpose commercial truck.

The Jeep, which became the model for the Land Rover, was probably the most notable vehicle of the second world war, and surplus examples were available on the peace-time market in large numbers. It was the result of a United States Army specification for a light reconnaissance vehicle to carry three men and a 7.6mm machine gun, with a wheelbase of 80in, a track of 47in, four-wheel drive, and light enough to be manhandled.

The specification stipulated an incline approach angle (the slope of a bank it could climb without fouling) of 45 degrees, and a departure angle (a bank it could descend) of 35 degrees, together with the ability to wade through water 18in deep. When it was drawn up in 1940, the draft included a demand

that a prototype should be available in 49 days, and 69 production models had to be ready a month later. All but a handful of the 135 car manufacturers approached by the US Army Quartermaster Corps decided the task was impossible. The deadline was critical. It left no time for elaborate engineering.

The outcome was the quarter-ton 4x4 General Purpose (GP) vehicle, known as the Jeep. It served on every battlefront with almost every army and captured Jeeps were prized even by the Wehrmacht. The lusty 2.2-litre side-valve engine produced sufficient power for nearly 60mph and vigorous performance across rough country. By the end of the war, Ford had made 278,000, Willys 361,000, and an archetype was

created for tens of millions of 4x4 utility vehicles for the leisure market that developed in the second half of the twentieth century.

No such phenomenon entered the mind of Maurice Wilks in the grim circumstances of the 1940s, when a war-surplus Jeep went into service on his Anglesey farm. The demand for ex-army Jeeps seemed to prove a market existed, and the success of the Standard Motor Company's lightweight tractors suggested small agricultural trucks had export potential.

It looked as though a civilian Jeep might help Rover meet its export obligations and ensure its steel allocation. It might also fill the factory until the world returned to

normal and full-scale car production could be resumed.

Maurice Wilks set up a design team under his deputy, Robert Boyle, who selected five designers one of whom, Gordon Bashford, was sent off to buy two Jeeps. The first prototype was built before there was a Land Rover chassis available, so it used one of the Jeep frames with a Rover rear axle and springs, and a rather meek 48bhp, 1,389cc Rover 10 engine.

Since the production run was to be so short, the design had to be plain, and next to nothing spent on tooling. The model's brief life expectancy, and the small numbers that were expected to be made, did not make a case for heavy expenditure.

The effect of the truncated design phase, as with the Jeep, was to impose utter simplicity on the designers. The Land Rover, as Wilks called it, had to be simple to design and simple to make. In the event it was also simple to service, simple to repair and strong.

Its extraordinary cross-country performance, never surpassed by any of its commercial rivals for the best part of fifty years, came about as a result of getting the fundamentals right. It had a serviceable balance of weight and power, it had good traction and spring articulation, and

once it was in production underwent a conscientious, progressive programme of development and change. It was a process for which Rover was well equipped. It had been following the same precepts throughout the 1930s.

Using off-the-shelf components, the designers employed the production saloon gearbox. Even the steering wheel was a standard Rover spring-spoke, and almost the only new item found necessary was a transfer box to take the drive to the front axle. The axles were broadly similar, which was a useful economy. The transfer box was a two-range affair, allowing the driver to select four high gears for main road cruising and four low ones for haulage off-road.

The simple body, built almost entirely of flat panels, was easy to make without much tooling, and also easy to repair in the rough and tumble conditions Land Rovers were expected to endure. The first

prototypes had no doors, once again in the style of the Jeep, and a drop-down tailgate giving access to the load space behind the driving seat.

Once Rover's own chassis was ready, it too had a wheelbase of 80in, much the same ground clearance as a Jeep, and an approach angle of 45 degrees and a departure angle of 35 degrees. The first 40,000 production examples had four-wheel drive without a central differential.

With commendable resource, Rover fell back on another item in its inventory and put a freewheel in the front drive to get rid of tyre scrub. So although four-wheel drive was permanent in the sense that it was permanently engaged, it was temporary in suffering the front wheels to run at a different speed when necessary. The freewheel allowed them to run faster than the rears on corners. The disadvantage was that four-wheel drive needed to be as effective coming down hills as it was going up, so engine braking on early Land Rovers was transmitted through the rear wheels only. They had the resources of two-wheel drive alone to pick their way down a mountainside.

The system was replaced in 1950, when the first major changes to the Land Rover introduced a selectable system with a dog-clutch engagement, giving the driver the

option of two-wheel drive for main roads, or four-wheel drive. Any freewheeling was now confined to the front hubs, which were locked in four-wheel drive for crossing country.

It soon became apparent, by the way Land Rovers were selling, that the model had a future well beyond the short term visualised in 1947. The stout chassis proved capable of withstanding tremendous punishment. It had plain, straight box-section beams, stout crossmembers, semi-elliptic leaf springs, and instead of the rather weak 10hp engine, it was provided with the ioe 1,595cc four-cylinder from the P3 Rover 60.

It was a sophisticated power unit for what was primarily an agricultural vehicle. The Jeep's side-valve slogger was much more appropriate, but it implicated no development costs and no delays in going into production. All the management had to do was increase its manufacture by the appropriate number each week.

There was concern that the firm's steel allocation might only be sufficient to make 1,000 Land Rovers in 1948. But as orders flowed in from the Amsterdam show, and the Bath and West Show of May 1948, and farmers recognised the worth of such a versatile vehicle, its future was

Bulldog breed. Sir Winston Churchill in characteristic pose outside Chartwell. (left)

80in Station Wagon of 1948. Sales were poor; re-emerged 22 years later as Range Rover. (right)

Adaptable Land Rovers.
Military version stripped
for action with the SAS.
(above)

secured. The aluminium body, which was merely a convenience at first, proved an asset. The external hinges and corner strengthening fillets gave it a brawny air. Customers appreciated its rust resistance and the way it withstood the knocks and jolts of industry or agriculture.

One of the virtues of the rudimentary design, besides its energetic cross-country performance, was the Land Rover's adaptable nature. Once again the Jeep was the role model in encouraging the design of Power Take-Off (PTO) attachments. A shaft was added to the transfer gearbox for operating a winch, a compressor, a small electrical generator or a belt-drive for farming machinery.

The Land Rover Mobile Welder of

1948 was one of the first attempts at a specialist model, and although sales were slow, it showed the way for a succession of Land Rover fire engines, camper vans, snowploughs, police and military vehicles, small armoured cars, ambulances, riot control vehicles, overhead cable repair platforms, pick-up trucks, mobile workshops and personnel carriers.

It also opened the way for one of Land Rover's first commercial failures, with an excursion into the leisure market. This was the handsome Station Wagon, introduced in October 1948, with a body made of aluminium panels on a coachbuilt ash frame. It was a well-proportioned seven-seater, devised by Abbey Panels of Coventry, with a metal cover over the bonnet-mounted spare wheel. Sales proved disappointing and only 641 were made.

As a passenger car, it attracted purchase tax, making it twice the price of an ordinary open-bodied Land Rover. Yet it was not forgotten. The market was not ready for the Station Wagon in 1948, but a conviction remained with Rover that a well-equipped, even luxurious all-purpose vehicle would come in due course.

The development costs of specialised Land Rovers proved more than their

limited numbers were worth, and by 1952 work on them was mostly delegated to experts in the firefighting, ambulance, or commercial fields.

The continuing success of the Land Rover may have looked assured, but it took some time for the management to become convinced that its luck would hold. The company remained careful about committing investment, and failed to carry on installing the Land Rover's 4.88:1 axle after the cars ceased using it. Manufacturing two axle ratios appeared prodigal, so the Land Rover had to use the P3's 4.7:1 even though it made it less nimble on hills.

The modifications carried out in 1951 still chiefly used components from the car side of the business, but some investment became inescapable. The demand for more power for towing resulted in replacement of the old 1.6-litre engine with a 2-litre. It was essentially the same engine with larger-bore cylinders, and although it produced only 2bhp more, it offered substantially better low-speed pulling.

There were a few concessions to practicality, and the headlamps emerged from behind their mesh screen grille. They had been put there apparently to make them less vulnerable, but in reality because they could be small, unchromed and cheaper.

By 1954 Rover seemed persuaded the Land Rover was here to stay, and a new version of the 2-litre engine was put in hand, together with a stretch of the 80in wheelbase to 86in and the introduction of a 107in version.

For the first time a Land Rover could be bought in a colour other than green. The 1947 models were sage green, then dark green, but as part of the new strategy for 1954 customers could choose grey or blue as well.

Increased sales brought greater confidence in 1956, when the wheelbases grew by a further 2in to 88in and 109in, while body styles such as the long Station Wagon began to proliferate. The first diesel was a supercharged 2-litre twin-cylinder, made by Turner of Wolverhampton, later replaced by Rover's own four-cylinder with Ricardo Comet combustion chambers.

The confidence was well placed. In its first ten years twice as many Land Rovers were sold as Rover saloons - 200,000 against 100,000 - and the company's survival was assured.

Further developments followed. There were many military Land Rovers, among them versions developed for carrying by air. There were lightweight Land Rovers, which could be slung under helicopters, and forward control Land Rovers for pulling guns. There were Land Rovers with the rear wheels driving tracks, amphibious Land Rovers, armoured Land Rovers, Land Rovers made in Belgium for the Belgian army, Land Rovers made in Germany for the German police, and Land Rovers made in Spain.

Military connections came to mean so much to Land Rover that by the 1990s the basic model was known as the Defender. It was a long way on from the US Army's 4x4 quarter-ton GP, and even managed to defy the recession of 1991-1992, when production never slackened from 320 a week at a time when almost every other sector of the industry was cutting back.

Land Rover expeditions flourished, and there were so many requests for information on taking Land Rovers to remote parts of the world that the firm published *A Guide to Land*

Rover Expeditions. The real purpose behind the modest booklet, besides offering sound advice for travel to implausible destinations, was to head off the entreaties that arrived almost weekly for free vehicles for deserving exploration teams. A constant flow reached Solihull from universities, adventure clubs and safari organisers. The guide was usually as much as they received, with information on the relative merits of petrol or diesel engines, a list of desirable extras, tools, spares and equipment, based on the accumulated experience of hundreds of fellow-trekkers.

There was fine detail aplenty, such as the importance of passport photographs to keep world-wide bureaucrats happy, and the ambient temperatures at which Land Rovers could normally be started and

Adaptable Land Rovers. Equipped with caterpillar tracks for boggy ground. (above)

Business-like interior of a six-cylinder 109in Land Rover. (left)

Bluehills Mine, Cornwall,
Range Rover raises dust
on the press launch in
June 1970.
(above)

*washing powder. After 100 miles
they should be clean.'*

The booklet also explained: '*The
Land Rover has been associated with
expeditions for many years and the
publicity we can gain from these
ventures is now very minimal.
Consequently, as a rule, any request
for monetary or material assistance
will not be considered.'*

Land Rover considered tuition in
off-road driving as important, not
only as a stimulant to sales, but
as something of a responsibility.
A testing track, laid down within
the boundaries of the Solihull
factory, developed into one of the
world's best compact off-road
courses. Customers were offered
tuition on climbing, wading, and
driving over obstacles. The facility
included a jungle trail where drivers
faced two feet or more of water,
earth banks with alarming 47
per cent side tilts, and even a flight
of steps.

Members of the presentations and
demonstrations team, such as Roger
Crathorne and Don Green, were able
to establish the Land Rover's
superiority by tackling obstructions
which appeared impossible for
anything with wheels. Courses were
run for drivers from the emergency
services, on the track where the Land
Rover, Range Rover and Discovery
were all developed.

operated. There was advice on what
to take, what to leave behind, and
where to put things. '*Front-mounted
jerricans should not be used to carry
fuel due to the fire hazard in the
event of an accident'*, it said.

There were injunctions about

looking inside sleeping bags for
scorpions, and advice on washing
clothes while travelling, tacitly
admitting that a Land Rover's ride
could be somewhat agitated. '*Put
them in a waterproof, sealed
container in the back of the vehicle
with a suitable amount of water and*

Range Rover chassis
showing transfer gear to
drive shafts, V-8 engine,
coil-spring suspension.
(top right)

Range Rover interior
designed to be
hosed down.
(below right)

Further changes to the Land Rover's engineering came with the addition of the six-cylinder engine in 1966 and the V-8 in 1980, marking the return to permanent four-wheel drive, which distinguished it from many of its rivals. Among the innovations were a locking centre differential and long-travel coil springs.

The initiative for the redesign followed the launch in 1970 of the logical successor to the pioneering Station Wagon of 1948. There was never any doubt that a market for a luxury Land Rover existed - sales to sporting estates told their own story.

The defeat of the Station Wagon only came about as a result of the purchase tax regulations. Its encouraging reception by the press and dealers brought about a 1952 resolve to look at the market again. A programme was put in hand for a vehicle tentatively called the Road Rover, a large estate car with rear-wheel drive only. Various proposals reached a running prototype stage but none achieved production. They were generally bulky, heavy and grew unwieldy during development. By 1960 the Road Rover was in abeyance.

Instead Spen King and Gordon Bashford embarked on a new kind of four-wheel-drive vehicle. They remained convinced of a demand for

a Land Rover that placed more emphasis on good road behaviour than off-road ability, and drew up a plan for something tentatively called the 100 Inch Station Wagon.

The basis was a strong Land Rover-style chassis and a separate

aluminium body, with long-travel coil spring suspension to provide a better ride, without relinquishing the Land Rover's cross-country grip. It had closed bodywork and the appointments of a saloon car. The aluminium V-8 engine, acquired in the 1960s, provided the power for

Almost alone to
increase production in
the slump of the 1990s,
Land Rover owed much
of its success
to Discovery.
(right)

Novel interior.
(above)

the necessary speed, and by the late 1960s all the ingredients for the Range Rover were in place.

Resources for development were slim at first, because the firm was preoccupied with new saloon cars, and King took responsibility for styling as well as engineering. The result was inspired. The proportions were right, the performance spectacular, and when King passed the project to David Bache for finishing in 1967 only detail changes proved necessary. Bache fine-tuned and indented the panel along the body sides, added the strikingly practical interior, and except for minor embellishments the job was complete.

The Range Rover was launched as a single model to an enthusiastic press and public in 1970, setting an industry benchmark for dual-purpose four-wheel-drive vehicles. It was 1981 before there was a five-door model, 1983 before the transfer gear whine was eliminated, and 1989 before it was joined by the equally innovative and less expensive V-8 petrol and four-cylinder diesel Discovery.

The Range Rover was the first production vehicle anywhere to provide an easy 90mph on the road, together with convincing cross-country performance. It was an astonishing achievement. The quality

of the ride, a substantial improvement on the Land Rover, was far more smooth and level than any cross-country 4x4 ever. Its tyres were remarkable Michelins as effective at motorway speeds as climbing muddy slopes.

The only quality that eluded them was silence. Treads deep enough for biting through mud or clay and strong enough for climbing over rocks proved noisy.

It was three years before the Range Rover was offered with power steering. The first rendition was accordingly heavy to park, and hydraulic assistance was needed to earn the endorsement of small drivers of either sex. The vigorous V-8 made the Range Rover a formidable towing vehicle. It proved ideal for pulling horse-boxes, boat-trailers or caravans from the gymkhana field, slipway or camping ground.

The basic box-section chassis and aluminium body survived three main revisions. In the middle of 1981, engine power was increased, automatic transmission (Chrysler Torqueflite for two years, then a ZF 4HP22) became available in 1983, and in 1984 there were bodywork revisions and a restyled facia. Not all the body changes were welcomed by the Range Rover's customers, notably the replacement of the wide

door handles that could be operated with gloved hands in freezing weather with small ones.

In September 1985 the 165bhp fuel-injected Vogue model took the Range Rover into the world of 'haute couture'. It was named after the well-known fashion magazine, and aimed at a wealthy leisure market. In April 1986 the VM turbocharged diesel injected a more practical note into the production, now taking place at the newly equipped Solihull North factory.

Neither the five-speed gearbox of 1983 nor the fuel injection of 1985 did much to improve petrol consumption, which was on the heavy side for a car although not excessive for a load-carrier.

The Range Rover was in production for 22 years before the next important engineering revision. This was a lengthening of the wheelbase and an increase in engine power to 200bhp from a 4.2-litre version of the evergreen V-8. The wheelbase was stretched by 8in, totally dedicated to extra space in the back.

The steel coil springs were replaced by air springs for the 1993 Vogue LSE, the wheelbase stretched to 108in, and the interior made even more luxurious. The price went up, too, to £40,000, but with the leather upholstery, air-conditioning and rich

furnishings, the Range Rover suffered no rivals in the four-wheel-drive market in either Europe or the United States, where it was relaunched.

The engine may have been uprated, but the significant changes were electronic air suspension (EAS) and an electronic traction control system which began a new era in four-wheel-drive vehicles.

The five height settings of the EAS system spanned a range of 130mm. In the middle was a standard position for normal road use up to 50mph, giving the same ride height as the metal springs. Above this speed the suspension dropped 20mm to improve aerodynamics.

For off-road use the driver could select a position 40mm above standard for negotiating rough ground or wading. This could increase by a further 30mm for pulling the vehicle out of boggy soil, or when it was grounded on rocks with the wheels spinning.

Access mode lowered the Range Rover 60mm below standard to make getting in and out easier. The electronic control unit (ECU) received signals from the height sensors, and took information about road speed, engine speed, the footbrake, handbrake, the automatic transmission selector, and the door-

closing switches so that, for example, access mode was not selected when somebody was getting in or out, or the vehicle moving.

EAS almost provided the Range Rover with the ride quality of a car, without losing any of its off-road capability. More important, the complex system of air compressor, air drier, electronics, and 10-litre air reservoir inside the lefthand chassis rail maintained its equilibrium regardless of load.

In moving even further upmarket the Range Rover also developed a good deal more legroom in the back, providing the lounging space that went with the increased wheelbase. The ride on the road turned out little better than that of a steel-sprung Range Rover, but its hoisting and lowering abilities gave it a further advantage over other four-wheel-drive vehicles, especially in the American market. Like Rover, Land Rover had a successful slogan, 'The Best 4x4 by Far'.

Whether the Range Rover gained its success through a triumph of image-making and marketing, or an accident of fashion, was inconsequential. It was equally at ease at the point to point as outside the Savoy. Like the Mini, it transcended boundaries of class and seniority, at least throughout the 1970s. In due course it gained

something of a reputation with what came to be known as Chelsea farmers, a derisory term for town dwellers who enjoyed the cachet of country style but rarely ventured beyond London's M25 orbital motorway.

The Range Rover's principles changed little for the best part of twenty years. The strong box-section chassis remained the same and only the options changed. A five-speed gearbox, automatic transmission, a turbocharged diesel engine, and the towbars and winches that were such a vital feature of the Land Rover were all available. Air-conditioning came in, and the trim was altered from the rural and hard wearing to explicit richness.

The seats of the first Range Rovers were made in a moulded plastic material, which looked like a robust sort of leather, and the floor was covered in stout rubberised matting. It was designed, according to the publicity of the time, to be hosed out if necessary. It was not seen then as

the luxurious limousine-alternative that it became; it was more of a slightly posh but still severely practical Land Rover.

The facia was modest and functional but David Bache, with customary deftness, gave it the appearance of a down-to-earth flight deck. It was a Rover that from the start was finely adjusted to its market and brooked no opposition. It was unique.

In due course its emphasis shifted. The moulded pleated seats gave way to something more effete, but it remained a masterpiece of detailed design, tailored with an exactitude that none of its imitators matched. There were no gimmicks. It did not hang its spare wheel outside. There was no need to make such a visual statement to reinforce its Jeep-like character. Its crisp silhouette and careful detailing said it all without any need for ornamentation.

It had such purpose and precision that one commentator compared it with NASA's lunar rover: *'An alien from another planet, starting from scratch to create the best possible vehicle for exploring Earth, would have had to come up with something like the Range Rover.'*

The demand for an ever more luxurious Range Rover opened up a gap between it and Land Rover, leading to the introduction of the

Discovery in 1989. In some senses Discovery inherited the mantle of the 88in Station Wagon of 1948; here was what Maurice Wilks and Spen King were thinking of in the 1960s when they conceived the 100 Inch Station Wagon.

Discovery fitted neatly into the rich middle ground of the four-wheel-drive market. Introduced at £15,750, or around half the price of a Range Rover, it was a cut above small Japanese jeeps, popular farm and leisure carry-alls with limited capacity and little luxury.

Cheaper than the Range Rover and the Mercedes-Benz Geländewagen, the Discovery was less rustic and challenged well-established Mitsubishi Shoguns, Nissan Patrols and Toyota Land Cruisers. Its significance in industry terms was to show that some Western motor manufacturers did remain capable of matching the Japanese.

The assets that made the Range Rover the best car in its class were retained for the Discovery. It had permanent four-wheel-drive, much the same stout chassis, aluminium body panels and supple springing. It also had agreeable styling, a useful degree of luxury, and it was roomier than a Range Rover. It had full-sized seats for seven and a tall load space, which could carry a chest of drawers or a small wardrobe.

It was more habitable than a Land Rover, car-like rather than agricultural, with high and low gear ranges providing a firm grip off-road. The price was the same for both the petrol V-8 or the exemplary 2.5-litre diesel, the Tdi, which promised 26-28mpg against the petrol's 18-20mpg. Its 19.5-gallon tank provided nearly 550 miles between refuelling stops.

The diesel was slower, but the addition of a turbocharger gave it a spirited performance and a top speed over 90mph. It was less quiet, but once up to speed the noise was lost in the swishing of the tyres, still an inescapable penalty of a usefully deep tread that did not clog with mud.

The Discovery's interior was a crisp attainment with bins for holding things, a detachable shoulder bag between the seats, and a large pouch behind the rear seat to hold the sunroof glass. Textures, materials and practicality were in the style and quality of the old 88in ash-framed Station Wagon of 1948.

The five-door Discovery did not become available until a year after the model's introduction. The tailgate hinged at the side instead of splitting horizontally like the Range Rover, and among the clever details was a radio that could be controlled from an alternative set of switches

within fingertip range. It had a comprehensive list of extras. The two folding seats at the back cost an additional £375, air-conditioning was available for £1,290, and a roof rack at £200, fitted neatly in the lowered part of the roof above the driver, like an old-fashioned station taxi.

Like the Defender, it too withstood the industry trauma of 1991-1992, increasing production at the height of the recession by 10% to more than 550 a week. The Range Rover went up from 350 to 370 a week.

Land Rover and Range Rover became generic terms as evocative as jeep. Only a handful of trade names, thermos or hoover perhaps, have entered the dictionary as part of the language. Common usage has added yet another: land rover, lower-case without a hyphen.

Limousine style of 1990s Range Rovers was not for hosing out when soiled. (far left)

Air springs provided range of accomplishments for leisured Range Rover drivers. (left)

CHAPTER X

Second Millennium: the 2000

The announcement of the Rover 2000 in October 1963 was greeted with dismay by its rivals, delight by its dealers and customers, and something approaching disbelief by the world's motor industry. Conservative to the point of appearing staid, with the possible exception of the Range Rover, nothing so radical and original had appeared from the company in living memory.

Rover underwent a metamorphosis in the 1950s. A new generation took over, and just as assuredly and confidently as the Wilks brothers stamped their character on Rover in the 1930s, so the new generation made their mark in the 1950s and 1960s. Maurice Wilks relinquished the job of chief engineer to Robert Boyle in 1956, and became joint managing director together with George Farmer. He supervised the P6 until shortly before its announcement and his death in 1963.

Spencer Wilks was appointed chairman, a position he held until retiring after more than thirty years with the company, also coincidentally just before the launch of the P6. He took the position of life president in 1967, following the Leyland merger, and held it until he died in 1971.

The management changes of the 1950s increased the influence of the brilliantly gifted cousins Peter Wilks and Spen King in the engineering field. Bache's design studio was also able to make itself felt under the new regime.

To such keen young men anything seemed possible, and among the prospects discussed were hydropneumatic suspension (the Citroën DS19 of 1956 profoundly influenced designers all over the world -Rover bought one in 1958) and rear engines.

It was 1957 before the specification of the P6 began to crystallise and the beginning of 1958 before firm decisions on it were taken. The car that emerged bore some relationship to the abandoned P5 proposals of 1953.

Rover now felt confident enough to embark on a project that would command a longer production run than anything contemplated hitherto.

Viking ship.
In the wheel-hub of a
Rover 200 Coupé.
(left)

A car of between 1.8- and 2-litres was drawn up, with a 103in wheelbase, retaining the traditional Rover virtues of noise suppression and level ride. It aimed to appeal to the new executive customer emerging into the enterprise culture generated by the post-Suez Conservative government.

Politics delayed the introduction of the P6. Central planning interventionism had not been forgotten in Whitehall. Rover needed a new factory to build the new car if it was to be made in large numbers, and wanted it to be in Solihull. The government wanted it built in an area of high unemployment. A compromise was worked out. Rover would have its new plant in Solihull in return for building a new gearbox factory in South Wales.

The contribution of the P6 to the history of the car is subtler than it seems. It turned out less of a landmark than its features suggested at the time, yet like the Citroën DS, whose style and detail remained unique to its day and age, the Rover 2000 showed that radical engineering could come to the aid of designers aiming at new standards of roadworthiness in a medium-sized car.

It was certainly the best-sprung car of its time, save only for the hydro-pneumatic Citroën. It rode better than any production car in the world with steel springs. It was quiet as Rover ideals demanded, it was smooth,

tastefully furnished, and it introduced drivers to the new discipline of ergonomics with switches shaped according to their function.

It had so many clear-cut and obvious merits that observers were left wondering why some of them had not been thought of before. The originality of the famous shin-bins, capacious pockets below the facia ahead of the front seat occupants, earned many plaudits. The shapely seats, the crisp although rather notchy gearshift, and the conspicuously high quality of construction earned it respect and admiration from everyone who drove it.

The P6 failed to win as much flattery by imitation as Issigonis's Mini however. The base unit construction was deeply admired by engineers the world over, but was rarely seen again. The sliding-joint De Dion rear axle was a masterpiece yet proved for the most part unrepeatable.

The rationale for the unusual front suspension, feeding its loads into the strong central part of the structure, was widely praised. It was designed to enable the engine compartment to accommodate a wide range of power units. The 3.5-litre V-8 fitted, but the projected gas turbine never materialised, and the bell-crank suspension remained unique.

The P6 was at once voted Car of the

Year by a distinguished international panel of motoring journalists. It went down in motoring folklore as a classic; clubs and societies were devoted to its preservation, and motoring celebrities such as the former editor of *The Autocar*, Peter Garnier, ran one as their personal car years after it was no longer made.

There were flaws. When it appeared, Rover devotees were less than rapturous about imitation wood, and although the upholstery was leather it had none of the hand-stitched richness of the P4 or P5. There was road noise, not enough to be called resonance, but sufficient to concern P4 owners about falling standards.

It took five years for the P6 to reach the market, which was a long time for a car that was not especially fast or even especially cheap. It sold for £1,264 including tax, so it competed with the Austin Westminster A110, BMW 1500, Citroën ID (the cut-price version of the DS), Fiat 2300, Humber Hawk IV, Jaguar 2.4 Mk2, and Wolseley 6/110. The Daimler V-8 was more expensive at £1,599, and the Mercedes-Benz 190 was £1,693.

The Triumph 2000 was cheaper at £1,095. It had a smoother six-cylinder engine than the Rover's rather rough little overhead cam four, but it was no real competition in other respects. At a time when a Vauxhall Cresta automatic cost £1,059 and a Ford

Designer's eye Rover 2000. Wooden model (below) dates from 1956-1957, developed into 1958 sketch (right) which turned the rear wing inwards and abandoned rear window overhang.

Zodiac Mark III automatic £1,113, the Rover 2000 was astonishingly good value. There was nothing to touch it at the price, and in the first-ever Car of the Year election it beat the Mercedes-Benz 600 by 76 points to 65 points, with the innovative but ultimately unsuccessful Hillman Imp third with 31 points.

The structural concept of the Rover 2000 was a base unit of a stressed steel skeleton, to which the mechanical components and unstressed painted skin panels were bolted. It was an idea put forward by Olaf Poppe when he was Rover's chief production engineer, but not executed until taken up again by Gordon Bashford in the 1950s.

Practical experiments with base units were made as early as 1952, using a P4 saloon as the dimensional model. By the middle of 1954 there was a mobile test rig, with P4 Rover 60 running gear and experimental independent strut suspension. So when firm proposals were made for the P6 towards the end of the 1950s, a well-developed base unit was already in hand.

The virtue of the base unit principle became clear to Citroën engineers working on the DS19 in the 1950s. It made the body extremely stiff and an ideal platform for supple springing: it also seemed to be suitable for the sort of long-lasting car to which Rover was committed, because the exterior body panels could be renewed when they

rusted, while the base unit could be made more rust resistant.

In practice things did not work out quite as well as expected, and while P6 Rovers continued to achieve long and productive lives, body rot proved quite capable of attacking the inner parts as well as the outers. Still, it could be made to last more easily than many monocoque contemporaries.

The base unit enabled styling changes to be made quickly and easily, and although Rover shunned Citroën's plastic panels, it did use aluminium for some of the body. Finally, the principle appealed to production engineering, because it meant that the vulnerable body panelling could be affixed as the final step in the production process.

The base unit of the P6 consisted of the central passenger section - roof frame, floor, windscreen pillars, door pillars and rear quarters - together with the inner panels of the boot and the engine compartment. The engine and transmission, suspension and wheels, interior trim and wiring harness were added. The car was virtually complete and given its first factory test drive before the body panels - outer sills, doors, boot lid, bonnet, wings, grille, light units and bumpers - were put in place.

In the world of might-have-been, the P6 and the Citroën DS might have

represented a new kind of car structure. The days of the separate chassis had gone as the logic of the monocoque asserted itself. It made more sense for a car to be all-of-a-piece, instead of a platform with a body on top like a 19th century coach.

The shortcomings of built-up hulls were well known. They tended to be noisy, and in many cases almost as heavy as the chassis and body structures they replaced. The P5 had to have its own mini-chassis sub-frame to deal with such difficulties.

The base unit was something in between. It was more than a chassis but less than a monocoque body shell. It seemed to meet most of the objections, because it did not carry reverberating road and engine noise,

overhead camshaft four-cylinder's square bore and stroke dimensions took advantage of a taxation structure that had been changed in 1947.

The ioe engine, designed for the old regime, was not abandoned lightly. It set a new standard for silence and smoothness, but it was manifestly out of date, large, heavy, expensive and no longer sufficiently powerful or economical.

The new 1,978cc engine abounded in artful features, such as containing the combustion chamber within a recess in the piston crown. Common enough in diesel engines, its advantages lay in better control over combustion chamber shape, compression ratio and firing balance. A five-bearing crankshaft and an aluminium cylinder head with the inlet tracts integrally cast were included in a specification which, if not exactly innovative, was at least state of the art. Power output was 90bhp at 5,000rpm.

The engine was perhaps the least successful feature of the car. The hydraulic tensioner for the camshaft drive-chain took time to apply pressure, and the start-up clatter drew attention to a unit that was not as refined as Rover owners had come to expect. They were suspicious enough of many of the car's new features, growing dubious about an engine that was distinctly audible and, compared with the P4, quite harsh.

The commotion from the engine might have been forgiven had the performance been better. Top speed of the 2000 was just over 100mph and it took over 14sec to reach 60mph. A BMW 1800TI took 11.3sec, and the Rover was comfortably left behind by its roomier and cheaper six-cylinder rival, the Triumph 2000, at 13.6sec.

The Motor was a staunch advocate of the Rover. '*Comfort is the keynote. We would put the ride in the top three amongst European cars irrespective of price. Since the handling, roadholding and general stability give both the driver and the passengers the utmost confidence, and the Dunlop disc brakes are exceptionally powerful, the mental aspect of comfort is covered as well as the physical side.*'

like a hull whose bulkheads and large panels acted as sounding-boards. The unstressed body panels were easy to replace in the event of accidental damage.

Among the disadvantages were increased weight against that of a true monocoque. Since the outer cladding carried no stresses, the inner members that did had to be made thicker and heavier. Only the roof, held in place by close-spaced bolts, carried any burden.

The main beam loads were shouldered by the inner sills and the deep transmission tunnel. The engine

compartment and boot formed strong boxes, buttressed by the scuttle and bulkhead at the front, and the rear bulkhead formed the anchorage for the ingenious rear suspension.

The designers' resourcefulness seemed boundless. The deep box member reinforcing the scuttle, carrying the loads of the front suspension, also formed the hot air duct for the interior heater. Skilled door fitting was simplified by mounting the doors on a new sort of ballpoint hinge.

Providing a suitable engine for the P6 was problematical. The chain-driven

Wooden mock-up for Rover 2000. Instrument dials on facia shelf later changed to rectangular box. (left)

Fine proportons of finished car. (right)

'One has the impression that the car was planned by engineers who are enthusiastic drivers and by stylists who put function before decoration, and the result is something of an object lesson to other manufacturers.'

Alas, *The Motor* did discover the 2000's Achilles heel. '*In refinement our test car fell a little below the very high standard set by previous Rovers. It is a quiet car generally, particularly at high speeds, but when travelling slowly tyre noise can be prominent on some bad surfaces. The gearbox too could well be less audible in second and third speeds, and the engine becomes fussy well before its generous 6,000rpm limit is reached. We have to make these remarks on the evidence of two pre-production examples, although we are* well aware that substantial improvements may have been made by the time production cars reach the public.'

It was a pious hope. The five years it had taken the 2000 to reach the customers were long enough to get rid of the engine noise, had there been any practical means of doing so. The P6 had to live with its blemishes. The engine remained noisy and the whines never really went away, a penalty it seemed of Rover at long last moving over to synchromesh not just on second gear, but bottom as well. Fortunately the advantages remained, in particular the supple ride, which was owed to a remarkable combination of luck and judgement by Bashford, Peter Wilks and King. They had to take account of a requirement to exploit the superior road grip attainable by the new radial-ply tyres. A new set of techniques had to be established to deal with such tyres; the suspension had to be compliant in new directions and chassis stiffness was at a premium.

Among the prerequisites was that the P6 should be capable of accommodating a gas turbine engine should there be a breakthrough in its development. It soon became apparent that this was unlikely, but by then much of the work on the novel front suspension had been done. Principles were laid down conveying the suspension loads into the stiff central section of the body. It was more trouble than it was worth to change, and the arrangement did contain some useful advantages, notably the safety associated with such a short steering column.

To make room for a fat turbine, the engine bay was made as wide as possible, so the front suspension was, in effect, turned through 90 degrees. It was pivoted on the front bulkhead, and the coil springs were mounted horizontally under the front wings, operated by way of upper links acting as rocking levers. These were attached to upright kingposts, acting on the wheel hub, and by pushrod to the spring.

Wheel location was by means of two radius arms, and the shock absorbers were mounted on the upper links, close by the springs. The steering column was a short affair, terminating at an Adamant-Marles hourglass steering box on the scuttle, linked by means of a horizontal idler lever and hydraulic steering damper by drag links to the wheels. The entire engine bay was free of any sort of encumbrance.

It was an elegant solution to a problem that in the event was never posed. A more conventional system would have done just as well, and been cheaper so far as the 2-litre four-cylinder engine was concerned, as well as the projected five-cylinder or even V-6 that were in the designers' minds.

Bache at his brilliant best, first V-8 P6s had the 2000's binnacle box. (below)

Wide tyres and broad shoulders of 4.3-litre V-8 development car converted for racing. Bonnet intake gulps air for four double-choke Weber carburettors. (right)

What was not in their understanding, until the eve of the 2000's announcement in October 1963, was a 3.5-litre V-8. When William Martin-Hurst ran his tape measure over the little aluminium masterpiece on the floor of Mercury Marine's boatyard in Wisconsin, this was the clear unencumbered engine compartment he had in mind.

At the back, a De Dion axle of exquisite design matched the inventiveness shown at the front.

The De Dion principle, named after a French marquis but almost certainly not invented by him, consisted of a light tubular axle linking the rear wheels. It was curved round the final drive unit firmly fixed to the chassis, and the drive was taken to the wheels by separate jointed half-shafts.

Its advantage was that it kept the rear wheels upright; its disadvantages were those of any non-rigid rear springing, namely the difficulty of driving wheels that were constantly on the move in relation to the chassis. Although they remained parallel, they had an erratic relationship with the final drive.

The problem was gracefully solved on the P6. A sliding joint was built into the De Dion tube to accommodate the sideways movement as the wheels described their arcs. The result was that the half-shafts could be of fixed length, and no longer had to embody

sliding joints prone to lock-up under power. They could act as locating arms for the rear wheels. Fore and aft location was provided by a Watts linkage which also formed the spring carriers, and in a further contribution to reducing unsprung weight, the rear brake discs were carried inboard beside the final drive.

The Motor was not the only reviewer ecstatic about the ride and handling of the Rover 2000. The Autocar found that 'Over average roads it is quite practical for passengers to read or even write with very little disturbance. When cornered fast the car heels over very little and the seats provide good lateral support, all of which makes for *unusually fatigue-free travel. Driven near the limit of tyre adhesion it handles like a well-bred sports car, a slight understeer finally predominating, and in the wet the light unsprung weight of the De Dion axle pays safety dividends in good traction and freedom from unpredictable skidding.'*

Bache's interior was as masterly as the rest of the car. The instruments were grouped together tidily in a box ahead of the driver with a strip-type speedometer, which proved unpopular and was later changed. The steering wheel was adjustable for height, an advantage conferred by the short steering column and a rare feature at the time. Unusual, too, was the deep transmission tunnel and central console dividing the front compartment. It prevented *The Autocar*'s testers from '... *slipping across easily to use the passenger's door in a home garage or crowded shopping street'*.

Shaping switches according to their function was just as radical, and the Rover 2000 was one of the first cars to use multi-purpose stalks, placed behind the steering wheel. The right one operated the horn by pulling it back, and the direction flashers, by moving it up and down. The left one flashed the headlights or dipped them at night.

Rocker switches were hooked, rotating ones T-shaped, and push-pull ones

round. Bache also saw no reason to pretend that a car 50in wide at shoulder height and 55.5in at hip level seated five people. Accordingly he shaped the rear seats to show that they were intended to carry two in comfort like those in the front.

Rover showed its sturdy independence, and indifference to fashion when it got in the way of practicality, by offering as an alternative mounting for the spare wheel upright at the side of the luggage boot, a carrier that mounted it externally on the boot lid.

During its development testing, the P6 was badged as a Talago, an invented name from the initials of T L Gawronski, the P6 project engineer. A Talago Motor Company was registered so that the name would even appear on the tax disc. Driving pre-production prototypes in public before launch day, *The Motor* test staff was surprised to discover how little stir they created, in contrast to the usual knot of people who clustered round an unusual or striking-looking car.

'Most people probably summed it up as Italian, expensive, and unattainable' was as profound a compliment as *The Motor* could confer in 1963.

The styling programme started with some radical concepts from David Bache. His brief was to make innovations that would make a car appeal to a younger clientele, a new

sort of customer who wanted something smart and practical but would likely adhere to the idea that wood and leather interiors were part of the executive style.

Bache had to design for a new phenomenon in the market. The Rover 2000 was perhaps the first car in the world for what came to be known as the executive market. The first prototype had a drooping nose with two headlights in faired pods. The young designers were forced to concede a radiator grille and four headlights.

The fine handling and roadholding of the 2000 quickly led to calls for more speed. The new engines in the car's development programme proved slow, and when the V-8 entered the picture, the five- and six-cylinder alternatives were quickly discarded. The first intimation that there was more power available came at the Geneva motor show in 1966, with the twin carburettor 2000TC, which gave acceleration to 60mph in 11.9sec and a top speed of 110mph at the expense of some engine harshness and a deterioration in fuel consumption.

The 2000 was notably economical, giving between 23 and 25mpg. The extra carburettor brought a penalty of 2-3mpg, not enough to deter export customers, to whom the extra speed proved more important than the loss of refinement.

Egg-crate grille of 1972 Mark II TC. (right)

More significantly for the future of the car, and the fortunes of the company, was its integration in 1966-1967 into the British Leyland Motor Corporation. Leyland already controlled Standard-Triumph, which had far-reaching implications for both the P6, and its long-standing rivalry with the Triumph 2000. By 1971 the conflict of interests under the Leyland umbrella seemed inappropriate, and the Rover and Triumph operations were for most purposes combined.

The practical results included a reappraisal of the P6 programme. Development of the V-8 went ahead together with a large number of alterations, many of them cosmetic, as the new corporation tried to pull itself together.

In the hiatus the Triumph was enlarged to 2.5-litres, given Lucas fuel injection, and underwent an unhappy elongating restyling by Michelotti in 1969. Quality control difficulties hastened its demise, together with the ill-starred Stag in 1977.

The Rover, meanwhile, was enlarged to 2.2-litres and if the American market had believed all that *Car and Driver* told it in May 1966 it would have bought 75,000 cars a year. '*We have driven a Rover 2000TC for nearly 3,000 miles, on all kinds of roads and in every kind of weather, and we believe it is absolutely the best sedan that has ever been presented in the*

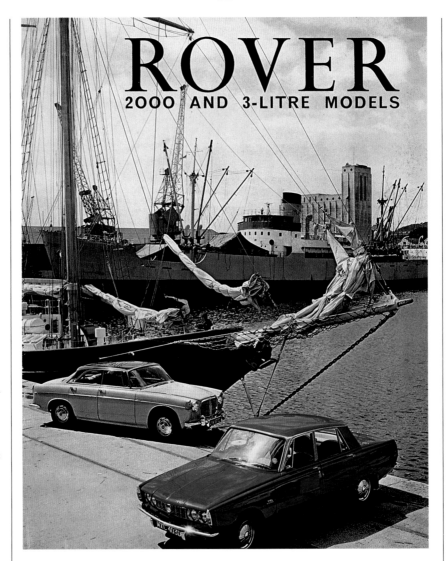

2000 TC and 3 Litre Rovers were complementary. (left)

pages of this magazine. We think it is an automotive milestone.'

Car and Driver, unfortunately, was ahead of the view of the man in the American street, who did not flock to Rover showrooms. There was vigorous promotion of the car's safety features in the wake of Ralph Nader's campaign, and the introduction of the United States Federal Safety Standards in 1968, but US sales stalled.

There seemed more hope for the V-8

North American 3500s
had elaborate air scoops,
wheel trims and an Icelert
frost-warning sensor.
(right)

3500, named oddly just before its launch in April 1968 the Three Thousand Five, to avoid confusion with the P5 3.5-litre, which remained in production until 1973.

Adapting the engine to fit was not difficult. It was tilted slightly to line up with the transmission housing, the front cross-member was moved forwards, and the battery rehoused in the boot. There were no major changes to the presswork and very little change in the weight bearing on the front wheels.

The gearbox was clearly not up to the job of transmitting 184bhp against even the 2200TC's 115bhp, so several development cars were equipped with five-speed gearboxes, made by the German Zahnradfabrik Friedrichshafen (ZF) firm. A Triumph gearbox was also tried, but neither proved suitable, so the car went on sale with automatic transmission only. The logic of the decision was that the market was moving towards automatics, and almost any manual gearbox capable of taking the strain would be heavy and disagreeable.

A special edition was made for the North American market, with bonnet louvres and fancy brightwork, but it met with very little more success than the TC. Emission control equipment, power steering, and air-conditioning soaked up a good deal of the available power, and some of America's

allocation of lefthand drive cars were brought back and sold in Europe instead. A manual transmission was developed for 1971, which gave the 3500 the energy it needed to reach 60mph in 9.0sec, and a top speed of 120mph.

The P6 was Rover's only credible competition car in the 1960s. William Martin-Hurst, inspired perhaps by the achievements of Mercedes-Benz in gaining its touring cars a reputation for speed and endurance in long-distance rallies, set up a competitions department. The new younger market that Rover sought was indeed impressed by P5 saloons showing that they were capable of astonishing performances, in some of the toughest events in the world, such as the East African Safari rally.

Martin-Hurst put Ralph Nash in charge, and shrewdly backed a team in the 1962 Safari, entered by the East African distributor. Two cars were put out by accidents, but two more finished third and fifth in the over

2,500cc class, and came 25th and 31st out of 45 finishers. Reaching the finish of a Safari rally, on the first attempt by large luxury saloons, was a major achievement. The cars' strength and reliability were impressive.

Private entries of cars prepared by the competitions department was a convenient ploy to deflect opprobrium when things went wrong, and reap the benefit of any success. In the Liège-Sofia-Liège Marathon de la Route of 1962, Ken James and Mike Hughes finished sixth and won the class, and Bill Bengry and David Skeffington completed the course an extremely creditable 18th. Once again, merely to finish was an impressive perfomance for such a large car - sixth place and a class win was astonishing.

Later in the year, to emphasise their triumph, James and Hughes finished 11th and came third in the over 1,600cc Touring class in the RAC Rally. A stirring display of reliability gave the works cars third place in the manufacturers' team contest. Bengry and a local driver, G E Goby, again completed the course in the 1963 Safari.

Rover was returning to successful competition for the first time since 1907, but although the fine record continued throughout 1963, brave displays of reliability were not enough. Work to adapt the 2000 for motoring sport was well under way when Jim

Porter took charge of the competitions department in 1965. Success followed almost at once, with a brilliant new driver who had partnered Richard Martin-Hurst, son of the managing director, on the 1964 Acropolis rally.

Roger Clark, with Jim Porter as his co-driver, took sixth place in the 1965 Monte Carlo rally behind Timo Makinen in a Mini Cooper, Eugen Bohringer in a Porsche 904, Pat Moss in a Saab 96, Peter Harper in a Sunbeam Tiger, and Herbert Linge in a Porsche 911. Only 22 crews finished the route in one of the toughest winter rallies for years, the Rover winning the Group One Touring category.

Clark's brilliant performance took him to greater successes with more competitive cars, and the 2000 never quite attained such fortune again. Yet it was established as a spirited sporting car and that, so far as Martin-Hurst Senior was concerned, was what mattered. The car went on to some notable performances in the Circuit of Ireland, the Welsh Rally, the RAC and the Scottish Rally, where it had the advantage of local knowledge of the notable Stirling driver Logan Morrison and his co-driver Johnstone Syer, who took third place and won their class.

Another Scottish driver who was also to discover success, Andrew Cowan, with Brian Coyle as co-driver, finished third in the Alpine Rally and won the GT category with a 2000TC. Other

V-8 engine fitted nicely under P6's bonnet. (left)

Rovers finished 16th and 22nd. The significance of such gallant - but ultimately sterile in rallying terms - efforts was far-reaching. Rover was provided with a fresh, youthful and vigorous image matching the new generation at the engineering helm.

It became clear that if the car was to compete convincingly, a much more assertive programme had to be put in hand. The cars needed to be lighter and more powerful. Jim Porter and Geoff Mabbs finished 10th in the 1966 Monte, but the budget for a full rally programme with cars prepared to meet the opposition on level terms was formidable, and the competition department was closed.

Rover re-entered competition four

years later with a P6 3500 development car, equipped with a 4.3-litre Traco-Oldsmobile V-8, a distant relative of the ex-Buick engine. It had a formidable performance and achieved a good deal of success, including leading the works Porsches by three laps in the 1971 84 hours Marathon de la Route on the Nürburgring, until forced to retire with propellor shaft vibration.

Martin-Hurst's dedication to serviceable publicity earned Rover a unique distinction in motor racing history as the entrant of the first gas turbine car ever to finish a major race. In 1962 the Automobile Club de l'Ouest (ACO), invited the T4 gas turbine car to make an appearance at Le Mans, to coincide with the announcement of a new category for

Jackie Stewart took the wheel of Rover-BRM at Le Mans (right) together with Graham Hill. (below)

Roger Clark triumphed in the Monte Carlo Rally. (far right)

gas turbines in the 24 hour classic. There had been, since 1953, a formula that equated gas turbines against piston engines; now the ACO put up a prize of Ffr.2,500 for the first gas turbine car to cover a minimum distance of 3,600km at an average of 150kph (93.2mph).

It was quite a rational initiative. The 1950s and early 1960s saw a great deal of gas turbine activity. Fiat's 1954 gas turbine project was based on the sporty 8V and in America Chrysler developed the promising Turbine

Special. By 1962 Chrysler felt confident enough to produce a series of Dodge Turbo Darts for evaluation by customers.

What the ACO probably hoped for was a revival of Renault's gas turbine programme. The nationalised French firm built the world's fastest gas turbine car, L'Étoile Filante (Shooting Star), which attained 192mph on the Utah salt flats in 1956.

The official reason for excluding the gas turbine from the actual racing results was that the organisers had to waive their fuel-tank capacity regulations in order to accommodate the engine's thirst. This presupposed that the ACO knew in advance how much fuel the Rover-BRM would need. It could easily have stopped for fuel more often.

What worried the ACO was the old equivalency formula. The organising authorities had very little idea how

well it would work out in practice, and it was anxious to encourage a turbine to take part - but not race against piston-engined cars - to see if its arithmetic had been right. The gas turbine racing car was too specialised a project for the existing competitions department, and Martin-Hurst sought out Sir Alfred Owen, head of Rubery Owen, the Midlands components firm with which Rover had connections dating back to the dawn of the industry. The Owen Organisation's BRM racing cars were at the height of their success, bringing Graham Hill the 1962 world championship. They concluded an arrangement for a single-seater chassis, adapted to take a 150bhp 40,000rpm gas turbine engine in place of its 200bhp 11,000rpm 1.5-litre V-8, and made into a two-seat open sports car. It had a rather rudimentary body, made by another Owen firm, Motor Bodies.

The car was ready for the April 1963 Le Mans test week-end. Graham Hill and Richie Ginther lapped the 8.5 mile Circuit de la Sarthe at 111.24mph. It finished the race in June, covering 2,592.96 miles (4,172.91km) at a speed of 107.71mph (173.346kph), which would have given it eighth place and would have won it the race in 1958.

Rover missed Le Mans in 1964. A new body was built after David Bache complained that exposing anything as unbecoming as the 1963 car gave a poor image of Rover. His department

BRM chiefs
Raymond Mays on left and
Sir Alfred Owen.
(right)

Jackie Stewart and Graham
Hill (in helmets) confer in
the pits at Le Mans.
BRM 'Wilkie' Wilkinson
leans down from pit
counter while Rivers
Fletcher (centre) films.
(far right)

was made responsible for a replacement and William Towns, later an outstanding designer in his own right, got the job of creating it together with a former Bristol Aircraft aerodynamicist.

The ACO agreed on an equivalency of just under 2 litres so the car could compete in the race proper. Fuel consumption remained problematical, and the entry was withdrawn following the April test week-end after showing that with regulation-sized fuel tanks there was little hope of it doing any more than trail at the back of the field. New heat exchangers were needed, and with an excuse that the car met with an accident on its way back from the April test and could not be made ready, the entry was withdrawn.

The 1965 event proved something of a disappointment. Jackie Stewart

replaced Richie Ginther in the now smoothly shaped car, although Towns's clean lines were spoiled by large intakes gulping air into the over-hot engine bay. The heat exchangers did their job, and no more than a repetition of its 1963 performance would have brought it once again into 8th place.

It was not to be. Unwanted debris in the engine, probably from the break-up of the new heat exchangers, damaged the compressor and inlet guide vanes, led to overheating, and 10th was the best it could manage, at an average speed of 98.71mph (158.85kph).

The fuel consumption of 13.5mpg showed that the fuel consumption problem was well on the way to solution. It was the first gas turbine car to compete in an international motor race, the first to finish, and earned *The Motor* trophy for the best placed British car.

Although very little faster than the MGB in 11th place, the Rover-BRM raised the firm's profile throughout Europe. It appeared technically innovative and confident enough to display itself in a competitive environment.

The competition programme was a success. The new generation had their way. Betjeman's subaltern would have recognised their certain touch.

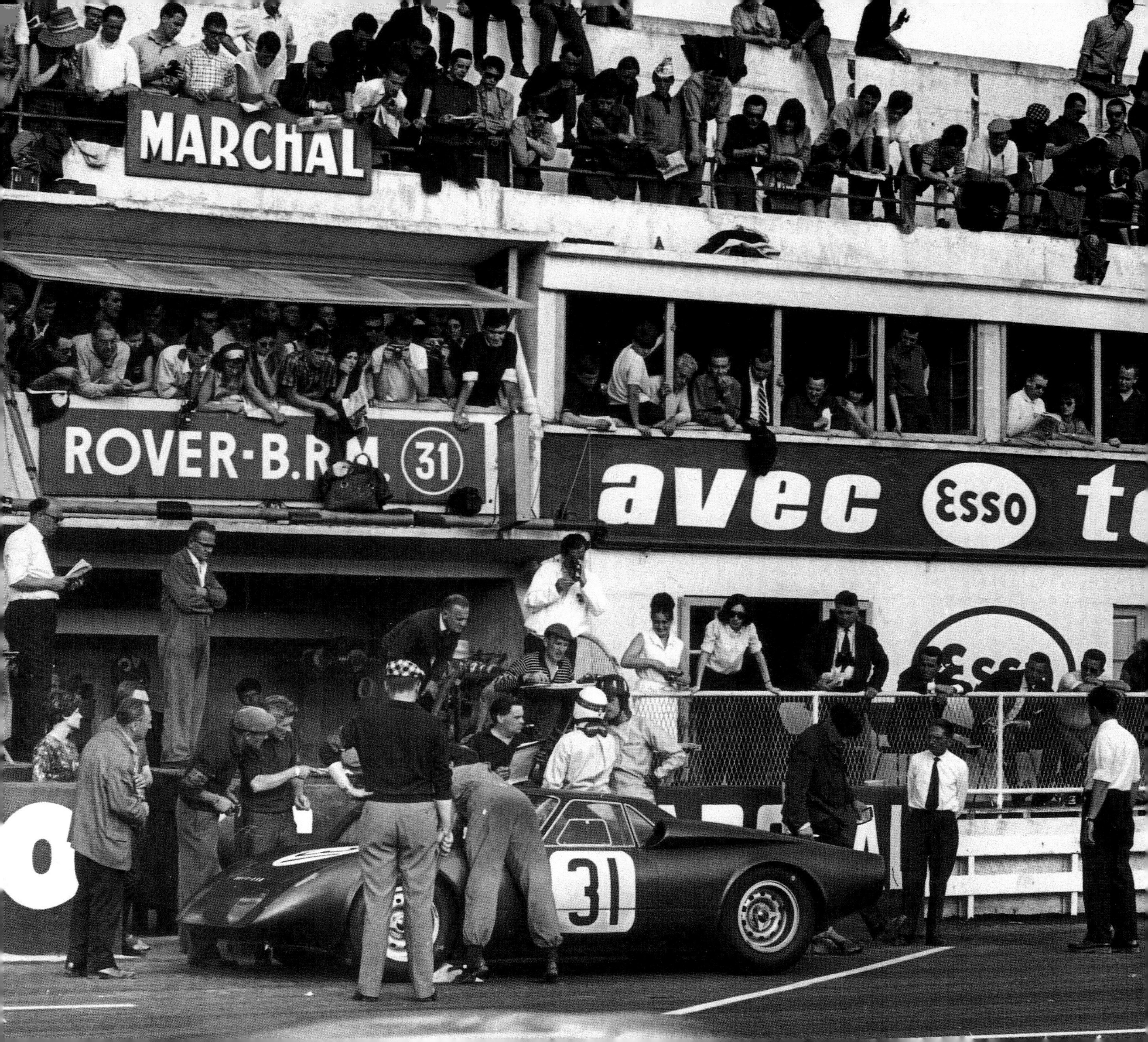
MARCHAL
ROVER-B.R.M. 31
avec Esso
31

CHAPTER XI

Car of the Year 1977

First thoughts on car that
would develop into the
SD1 by David Bache:
studio mock-up of 1971.
(above)

Specialist Division Project Number 1 (SD1) seemed, on the face of it, to be the antithesis of the P6. Rover appeared to be rejecting the P6's radicalism for a car that emerged at first sight prosaic. The SD1 had a five-door monocoque body, a live rear axle and Macpherson strut front suspension. Yet they were developed to a fine grade of excellence, and dynamically the car was a success. Alas, it never sold in the numbers it deserved, or was expected to.

It did at first. In the 1970s it outsold all previous Triumph and Rover models combined.

Had the SD1 come from a happy home it would have been a spectacular success. For ten years it sold well as a V-8, and with 2-, 2.3-, and 2.6-litre mutants, as well as a VM turbo-diesel. But its launch coincided with the upheavals of financial stress, takeovers, and the reorganisation of its parent holding company with the government as the main shareholder.

It lay at the end of a long road of mergers, cars planned and cars cancelled, during the industrial disturbances of the 1960s. The predicament that it ultimately resolved in the 1970s was largely a result of such turbulence. It was introduced in a fuel crisis, and played out its life in a state of industrial uncertainty that would have tested the most robust production.

Its tribulations were manifest, beginning with Rover and Triumph finding themselves in the same corporate empire. Both made cars in the same class, and the holding company had to make up its mind which to retain.

The SD1 was a product of the temporary collectivisation of the British motor industry. In the circumstances it was a surprise that it was made at all, astonishing that it was made so well. It would have been a miracle if it had been without blemish.

Historically the motor industry was composed of a few key players in the volume market, and a large number on the periphery making sports, luxury or specialist cars such as the Land Rover.

Ill-fated imaginative
mid-engined BS coupé.
(right)

The first big change took place in 1952, with the formation of the British Motor Corporation (BMC) from the Nuffield Group and Austin. In 1961 Leyland Motors, a successful truck and bus firm established in 1906, integrated with Standard-Triumph - itself the result of an amalgamation in 1945. Rover and Alvis happily merged in 1965 with quite modest ambitions to produce two compatible ranges of cars.

Within a few days of Rover and Alvis coming together, BMC announced that it was taking over Pressed Steel Ltd. Body manufacture was one of the lynch-pins of the industry. Only the biggest car makers could afford their own press shops.

The investment in heavy plant was beyond the resources of all but large-volume car makers, or an independent specialist such as Pressed Steel, whose plants at Cowley near Oxford and Linwood in Scotland supplied bodies to much of the motor industry outside BMC, including Rover and Jaguar. Paying for the dies that went into the press tools was as much as such relatively small companies could manage. Press shops of their own were out of the question.

The industrial equilibrium was maintained until 1966, when BMC acquired Jaguar and its partner Daimler, and formed British Motor Holdings (BMH). Leyland-Standard-Triumph and BMH were left

glowering at one another. Rover-Alvis, for its part, was suddenly vulnerable to pressure on its body-making facilities, since it could no longer be certain that BMH would continue the supply of bodies to a competitor of Jaguar.

Nobody in the motor industry ever forgot what happened in 1953, when the splendid Jowett Javelin suffered a hiatus in gearbox production. Unsold bodies piled up at its bodywork suppliers, Briggs Motor Bodies. During the ensuing difficulties, Briggs' new owners, Ford, lost patience and sold the plant near Doncaster. Jowett was left without a body shop, and collapsed.

Accordingly, in 1966 overtures from the Leyland group found a ready response, and the board commended them to Rover shareholders. Under Sir Henry Spurrier, Leyland had almost as long and distinguished a history in commercial vehicles as Rover had in cars. By March 1967 the arrangements were complete, and the companies were united.

Spencer Wilks, now 75, finished the job he began in 1930, and the new managing director, Sir George Farmer, revealed Rover's plans to the Leyland board and its chief executive, Sir Donald Stokes. They included the Range Rover, a remarkable coupé known as the P6BS, and a replacement saloon car for the P5 and the P6. The P7 title had already been awarded to

some stillborn research projects, so the new undertaking was code-named P8.

Stokes's next move needed the approval of the government. By the beginning of 1968 the old BMC group was ailing. Its Austin and Morris cars were not selling well. They were technically novel but had a reputation for unreliability, and cost control was poor.

Stokes and Sir George Harriman, chairman of BMH, arranged for Leyland and British Motor Holdings to merge. The result consolidated most of the British motor industry outside Ford, Vauxhall and the former Rootes group of Hillman, Humber and Sunbeam-Talbot.

The new coalition was called the British Leyland Motor Corporation, and central to its plans in the specialist

Architects of consolidation of the greater part of British motor industry in the 1960s, Lord Stokes (below) and John Barber. (top right)

sector were Rover's Range Rover and P8. The P6BS coupé and a fastback P6, intended to be sold as Alvises, were so important to Rover's expansionist strategy that it looked as though they, too, would win approval.

When the new corporation was launched, on the eve of the announcement of P6B (the V-8 engined Three Thousand Five), they were already well in hand. But the dust created by the change in regime took a long time to settle. There had been a tacit assumption that since Triumph was one of the founding members of the Leyland group, it might be preferred as a luxury-market brand leader. Its sports cars were successful and high-profile, even if its saloons never quite attained the status of Rovers.

It was decided to keep both names in being, and set up a sort of in-house competition between the respective design teams to see which would be responsible for the larger of the two luxury cars planned.

A number of factors favoured Rover. The P5 3.5-litre had acquired a rare patina. It was not only the car of the managerial and professional classes, it was the car of royalty and prime ministers like Harold Wilson. The cabinet rarely alighted from Rolls-Royces or lengthy limousines - when it came to Downing Street it generally arrived by Rover.

Sir Donald Stokes and John Barber approved the outline plans for the P8, at the time of the Leyland-Rover merger in 1967. Both 2-litre and 3.5-litre versions were planned, but in an effort to raise the car's sights to the level of Jaguar and Mercedes-Benz S-Class, only the larger version went ahead. A 4.4-litre V-8 was proposed, and there was some satisfaction that none of the propositions thwarted any plans of Triumph.

The P8 was a base-unit design, like the P6, with a broad-shouldered, not to say massive appearance. The benefits of base-unit construction remained; the replaceable panels made accident repairs easier and cheaper. Early P6s were now old enough to show rust could take hold in both hold inner and outer structures, but the advantages in sound-absorption still held good.

Tooling was already in hand. Some £3 million had been spent already scheming for the production of a car, which had been brewing and maturing since 1964. The front suspension was a double wishbone, the rear a further refinement of the P6's De Dion, with jointed half-shafts. A hydraulic 'ring-main' supplied power to the brakes, steering and self-levelling suspension. King and Bashford created a stunning 130mph saloon, with the interior space of a P5 and the engineering integrity of a P6.

By 1968 full-size styling bucks for the

P8 were complete, production planning had begun, prototypes were running and a launch was planned for 1971.

It was not to be. The picture changed as soon as Jaguar joined the enlarged British Leyland Motor Corporation. The proliferation of competing models within the new organisation no longer made sense. Not only that, the combined profits were less than expected.

Plush interior of SD1 chauffeur limousine had writing desks and reading lights but no telephone or fax machine. (below)

Sales were more than £1,000 million, but pre-tax profits tumbled from over £40 million to less than £4 million. The cash investment demands at the volume end of the business came first, and the former Pressed Steel works at Cowley were retooled to make the Morris Marina. Extra money had to be raised, and there was not enough left to carry on with the P8 programme. Analysts estimated that between £3 million and £5 million had to be written off cancelling it.

Fortunately there was 75 years worth of goodwill behind Rover. The P5 could soldier on until 1973, and the Range Rover was launched to seal the success of the four-wheel-drive cars, which were to remain a cash-rich source of income through many years of changing fortunes.

The Mark 2 Rover 2000 was introduced in 1970, after 98,706 single-carburettor and 56,202 twin-carburettor cars were made. A radiator grille that resembled an egg-box and a lumpy bonnet were recognition features. After a further 24,603 SCs and 32,078 TCs, it was replaced by the 2200SC and 2200TC in 1973. The bigger-engined car lasted until 1976, and its total of 32,370 brought P6 four cylinder production to more than a quarter of a million cars.

The 3500 was similarly modified in 1970, and the 150bhp 3500S, capable of 122mph, introduced. Power steering

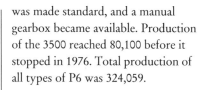

Reflections on SD1. Smooth body style radical for a big saloon. Frontal treatment inspired by Ferrari Daytona.
(left)

Car of the Year 1977. Handling and roadholding impressed international jury.
(below)

was made standard, and a manual gearbox became available. Production of the 3500 reached 80,100 before it stopped in 1976. Total production of all types of P6 was 324,059.

The cancellation of the P8 was a crushing blow to the hapless engineers in Rover's development department. To some it represented the culmination of their working lives. Worse was to come.

The P6BS and the Alvis GTS coupé also had to go. Prototypes of the pretty coupé based on the 2000 were already running and seemed certain of success; the astonishing mid-engined BS likewise held high promise.

Car manufacturers always engaged in projects that never reached production. Initiatives were taken to be ready in case of changing conditions. Economy cars conceived in times of plenty were made ready for introduction when a crisis broke. If the crisis went away, so did the plans.

Rover continued research on small cars. The aluminium industry did not forget the M-Type, and encouraged continued study of aluminium cars. Rover obliged with Energy Conservation Vehicle Number 3 (ECV 3), built by BL Technology Ltd at Gaydon in the 1970s. It had a bonded aluminium structure and flush-mounted windows, a three-cylinder overhead camshaft engine, and a smooth, aerodynamic body. There was accommodation for four in a vehicle based on Metro underpinnings.

It showed how energy could be conserved through weightsaving, and was used to demonstrate that for every 1% reduction in vehicle mass, fuel consumption improved by 0.3%. Later research put it even higher. By focussing weight reduction more towards saving fuel and less on simply going faster, ECV3 had the makings of a 100mpg car. The corollary was that an everyday car could be made with a smaller engine, smaller brakes and lighter components.

The mid-engined P6BS was planned to take advantage of the acquisition of Alvis. A sports Rover was inappropriate; a sports car carrying one of the greatest sporting reputations of the 1920s and 1930s would have been fitting and proper. Bringing the ingredients together was easy, starting with a powerful version of the V-8 engine.

The P6BS title sprang from a rather distant relationship with the P6, the B was added for Buick, and S for sports. The objective of putting the engine behind the driver but ahead of the rear wheels was good balance.

Rear-engined cars, such as the Volkswagen and the Porsche where it overhung the rear wheels, acquired a reputation for quirky handling. But

racing car designers of the 1950s overcame their prejudice, and discovered that placing it amidships gave drivers exactly what they wanted.

Weight was evenly distributed, a car could have equilibrium and symmetry. If a sports car was to mirror racing cars of the day, the engine had to be in the middle. P6BS was equipped with inclined SU carburettors under a plastic bubble behind the driving compartment, there was some luggage space above the transmission and a huge transverse silencer crammed in the back.

Fittingly for an Alvis, the BS, as it was usually known, was no rough and ready sports car. There was a strong emphasis on good ride and refinement. It was softly sprung with a De Dion

rear suspension based on the P6, and had 14in Minilite wheels at the front and 15in at the rear.

The prototype was secretly built at Alvis, with a serviceable closed coupé body. Styling studies were carried out, wood and clay models constructed with small rear seats and gull-wing doors like the 1952 Mercedes-Benz 300SL, and everybody who drove the car thought it admirable.

It was expected to sell at around the price of a Rover 2000 and was exhibited at the New York motor show in 1968. Alas, it looked like a threat to Jaguar and Triumph. It would have been £500 cheaper than a Jaguar E-Type, and Triumph had plans of its own to build a V-8 sporting coupé, the Stag of 1970.

Aluminium was used
extensively in ECV3,
developed at Gaydon
research centre
in 1981-1982.
(left)

Three-cylinder engine
promised up to 100mpg.
(right)

So the BS had to go. Rover engineering staff fought a rearguard action to put it on the road, but logic decreed that it had no place in the scheme of things, and it became another great might-have-been whose passing engineers and enthusiasts alike regretted.

Restrospectively it may have looked like a missed opportunity for a formidable sports car, but commercially it was inopportune and its cancellation almost inevitable.

The other victim was the Alvis GTS. The project name within the works, for David Bache's personal reaction to Rover's merger with Alvis, was 'Gladys'. On discovering that no replacement was planned for the ageing TF21, with its graceful coachbuilt Park Ward body, Bache designed a striking-looking car.

One of the virtues of the Rover 2000's base-unit structure was that reskinning was easy and relatively inexpensive -

even though it was never thought necessary. Using a P6 as a foundation, Bache's coupé had an innovative hatchback rear window like the newly introduced Renault 16. There were few external clues to its P6 ancestry; it was not badge-engineered in the way that led to BMC's downfall.

Unfortunately, the last thing British Leyland needed was yet another make of car. Austin, Austin-Healey, Daimler, Jaguar, MG, Morris, Riley, Rover, Triumph, Vanden Plas and Wolseley were enough to be going on with. Development work on both Alvises was discontinued. Bache nevertheless grew so attached to the GTS that he adopted the prototype as his own personal car.

Leyland resolved that its next corporate large saloon would supplant the Rover P5 3.5 and the P6 in all its forms, as well as the Triumph 2.5. Rover and Triumph designers accordingly drew up plans. Having abandoned the P8, Rover outlined the P10 (P9 was allocated to the aborted mid-engined car), Triumph the Puma. The P10 Gordon Bashford started work on first was another base-unit car. The cash for such an expensive platform was not available, and something simpler was demanded.

The P10 redrawn for introduction in 1976 had a monocoque shell and live axle rear suspension, and set the course for SD1.

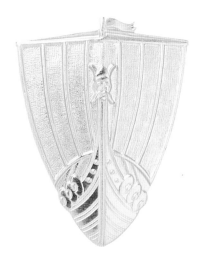

SD1 facia layout revised in
1982 with arc-type
speedometer and
tachometer.
(left)

Stylised symbolism of
Viking ship for the
1967-73 P5B grille badge.
(above)

Leyland's dilemma, which the SD1 solved, was how to fill the gap between Austin-Morris and Jaguar. The conflict between Rover and Triumph was plain, but so also, it seemed, was the answer. The breach should be filled with two cars, a 1.5- to 2-litre based on the Triumph 1300, and the 2- to 3.5-litre towards which both teams were working. Accordingly, the SD1 not only had to replace all the existing Rovers, but the Triumph 2000 as well.

Triumph's Puma was dropped, and the internal competition was decided in favour of the Rover styled by David Bache and engineered by Spen King. Corporate loyalty was important to Leyland as it sought to create an identity for itself, so as the design nominally came from the Specialist Division, it was given the title SD1.

Its first misfortune was to be a 3.5-litre, arriving in the wake of an oil crisis that rocked the social and economic fabric of the Western world. Announced in 1976, the Rover SD1 became Car of the Year in 1977, with 157 points, against the Audi 100 with 138 votes and the Ford Fiesta with 135.

It was the second time Rover had won the title, and it turned out to be a carefully appraised choice by the international jury of journalists. It did not prevail through its technical novelty or mass-market appeal, nor was it the sole big five-door luxury saloon of the time. It won through the maturity of its design, its superb handling and a unique stylishness.

It bore a striking resemblance to the Lancia Gamma, which had front-wheel drive, architecture by Pininfarina and a novel flat-four boxer engine. As hatchbacks, both broke new ground. A fifth rear door was still found mostly on small cars; a large luxury saloon with one seemed bold. The Rover's front was self-consciously modelled on a Ferrari Daytona. The rest was fresh as paint, the finish pure Rover, except that leather upholstery was no longer standard and the reassuring grain of polished timber was missing from the facia.

The main mechanical ingredient carried over was the V-8, by the mid-1970s well-proven, reliable, and already one of the world's great engines. An innovative five-speed gearbox was designed by old rival Triumph, another member of the still-new Leyland partnership.

The front suspension Macpherson struts were located by an anti-roll bar, and the rear axle was a torque tube with coil springs. The De Dion was rejected on grounds of expense, the space it occupied and its burdensome weight.

Instead, a ride-levelling unit was incorporated in the telescopic shock absorbers, and the axle held in place across the frame by a Watts Linkage.

Fore and aft it trailed on arms pivoted on the frame, locating it firmly yet pliably.

The explanation for the repudiation of the P6's unique base-unit structure and inboard disc brakes lay less with the design staff than with the new regime of an industry undergoing a transformation.

The SD1 had good aerodynamics. Its drag coefficient of 0.39 was suitable for a car aimed at the motor roads of the European market, to which Britain was firmly committed.

The interior was another accomplished David Bache composition, with his favourite instrument box on top of the facia shelf, deep reclining seats, a central console and carefully matched textures and materials.

Bache never underwent the high-profile promotion of Giugiaro or the international superstars of the great design houses. Yet as an in-house designer for Rover, he was every bit as much an arbiter of fashion, observed closely by the rest of the industry.

Bache's genius set trends widely imitated throughout the 1970s and 1980s. His P5, P6, Range Rover and now SD1 were exemplary, corresponding as flawlessly for their markets as the Wilks brothers' creations of the 1930s. Like Clegg, like the Wilkses, like Spen King and

Gordon Bashford, Bache gave form to a Rover that caught the mood of the customer in his time.

Features of the interiors Bache devised set examples followed and refined by designers in Europe and Japan. It said a good deal for his appreciation of form and proportion that he was able to introduce a steering wheel with a flattened rim to clear the driver's knees, almost without anyone noticing.

Subtlety and understatement were Rover's style. When Austin tried a similar ploy with the Allegro, promoting the 'square' so-called 'quartic' steering wheel, it was greeted with such derision it had to be withdrawn.

The 3500's handling was beautifully controlled, and the performance vivid. Its top speed of 124mph (200kph) was the fastest in its class. Acceleration to 60mph (100kph) occupied less than 9.0sec, matching rivals such as the 2.8-litre fuel injection Ford Granada and the Opel Senator. The Rover hit its new European targets with precision, just as earlier cars reached the heart of the British middle class in the 1930s. It had the strength and safety of a Volvo but more style. It had the practicality of a Renault 30 without being so uncomfortably plain. And it was cheaper than a Mercedes-Benz 280.

In 1979 the 3500, as the SD1 was known, was enhanced as the V-8S with

Distinctive Bache silhouette remained unchanged throughout life of SD1. (left)

added luxury and weight. On the credit side it had a supple ride, velvet upholstery and air-conditioning, and its high gearing made it one of the best long-distance touring cars of its time. On the debit side it had axle hop on bumpy roads, back axle location was poor under braking, and its reliability was suspect.

The best engine for the top model was self-evidently the aluminium V-8, but further down the range lay a problem. The Rover 2000-2200 engine now seemed heavy and costly. Also, in view of competition from the likes of BMW in the European market, a smooth-running six-cylinder was needed.

A new cylinder head and overhead camshaft would bring the Triumph engine up to date, but there was insufficient time for that. Launch took place with the V-8 alone, and the

Acclaim HLS showing
transverse engine
and front drive layout.
(above right)

New era;
Triumph Acclaims
leave Cowley
in October 1981.
(below right)

smaller-engined Rovers and Triumphs remained in production until a fresh engine was ready.

Introducing a new model in the 1970s was not like the 1930s. It was no longer a case of phasing in different plant and machinery during the annual break, and starting production of a new car when the workforce came back off holiday. A whole new factory was needed for SD1, and British Leyland had to find £27 million to build it. The new plant was purpose-made, landscaped carefully into its surroundings to the east of the existing works. Leyland spent a further £100 million on the new gearbox facility at Pengam in South Wales and a body construction works at Castle Bromwich.

In 1977 Sir Michael Edwardes took on the job of restructuring Leyland into Jaguar-Rover-Triumph and Austin-Morris. By the early 1980s the eight Leyland car assembly plants had been reduced to three and by 1985 Triumph and Morris were history.

Under Edwardes, and then Sir Graham Day, a good deal of disengagement and unravelling took place. Rover-Triumph remained profitable, and Jaguar regained its independence. The old corporation was slimmed down with some parts disposed of, and the core car-making business regained the title of its best asset, Rover.

It proceeded to get on with making a success of the SD1 and planning a recovery programme, as painstaking as that which followed the management shakeout of 1930. Spencer Wilks would surely have recognised the logic of the remedy that Edwardes called 'a product-led recovery'. Once again the need was urgent. Once again it was necessary to call in facilities from outside Rover. In 1930 it was Hillman in nearby Coventry. In 1981 it was Honda in Japan.

The first announcement called it rather discreetly 'a programme of collaboration', which it was. Soon it became apparent that the collaboration was working, and was likely to be long-term.

The first tangible effect on the cars was a statement in September 1980 that the

Honda Ballade would be produced in Britain. Public interest was intense. It was aware of the treasure invested in the creation of a plant to build the Metro, and also establish a new test track on a former RAF V-bomber base at Gaydon in Warwickshire.

In June 1981 Ray Horrocks, brought in from Ford to be chairman and chief executive, said the new Anglo-Japanese car was not to be regarded merely as a stop-gap. It was to be launched at Motorfair in October 1981 and was not introduced as a Rover. It was the Triumph Acclaim, and it struck a chord at once. It would remain a feature of the company's production "... *with 80 per cent British parts and 70 per cent of the ex-works price British until that can be raised to 100 per cent*", said Horrocks.

In the first stage, the engine, transmission and some of the difficult facia mouldings were brought in from Japan. Concerning Honda, Horrocks said somewhat cautiously:"*We have discovered we can work together, but nothing more tangible than that. The Acclaim provides Honda with a royalty on each car produced plus a 'window' into the European market.*"

Following an investment of £70 million at Cowley, including robotic welding gear, the first 200 or so pre-production Acclaims were off the line by mid-March, and by July production was in full swing. By the time of the

official announcement to the press at the beginning of September, some 6,000 cars were ready.

The waiting journalists at the Imperial Hotel, Torquay, felt a sense of occasion. The motor industry was steadily becoming an international affair, and here was the evidence. There was no gainsaying the car's Japanese origin, but there were clear advantages to be obtained from that. Japanese cars had such a reputation for reliability that its success seemed assured. The Acclaim would fail only if it was thoroughly disagreeable, which it was not. Honda's reputation as a sort of Oriental Mercedes-Benz was already secure after generations of beautifully engineered motorcycles, and a shorter but no less spectacular history making cars.

Many of the press still remembered Honda's first sports car, the S600 of 1966. Its jewel-like twin overhead cam four-cylinder engine was only 791cc, yet it had the ingredients of a racing engine. It had an inclined hemi-head, roller bearing crankshaft, four carburettors, and with 70bhp at 8,000rpm propelled the little car at 100mph.

The S600 was introduced just as Honda took its first steps into motor racing. A successful Formula 2 engine showed how determined Honda was to have its way in cars, much as it had in motorcycles. Significantly, some of

Evolutionary progress. 1984 Rover 213 Vanden Plas showed Honda influence. (above left)

1992 Rover 214i 16v reinstated Rover identity. (below left)

Hatchback rear of SD1 proved controversial feature. Loading luggage exposed rear passengers to weather. (right)

Honda's 1960s racing engineers occupied senior positions in the firm.

The press took comfort from knowing that Rover was dealing once again with engineers, practical men, and not accountants of whose manoeuvrings it had grown weary.

The Acclaim was modified from the Ballade for the UK and Europe; it gained more luxury. It was not very fast, had a less than perfectly smooth ride, and there was not much room in the back, but these proved no barriers to success.

There was a lively market among clients not interested in speed, who drove on smooth roads, rarely carried more than two people and demanded a car that was well made and reliable.

The Acclaim's virtues were soon apparent. It was quiet, well-made, reliable and well-proportioned. It was also well equipped, and even if the electric window lifts looked like an after-market accessory, they were a luxurious touch for a medium-sized car. Acclaims were also offered with Honda's exquisitely engineered miniature air-conditioning unit, an unheard-of luxury for a 1.3-litre.

If the Acclaim was a shock to the system and better than expected, the Rover 200 was eagerly anticipated but turned out less good than it might have been. The change of brand name was

strategic once the successor's credentials were established. Alterations to the suspension incorporated lessons from the Acclaim, which had been improved by MGB designer Don Hayter. Accordingly the 200 was expected to be rid of the Acclaim's obvious faults.

It was not. Disappointingly, the Rover 200 was no more than a Honda Ballade again, inheriting many of its shortcomings. There was still not enough room in the back, the ride was uneven, and to make things worse it had a high sill to the luggage boot. It was still dependable, the finish still luxurious for a middle-sized car, and with the right equipment it seemed almost a match for a small BMW, even if it was not much cheaper.

Its faults were assuaged later. The ride was tranquillised and the boot redesigned. Fastidious private owners made for the Rover 216 Vanden Plas,

with its rich equipment, comfortable front seats, nicely finished interior, and the prospect of trouble-free, economical motoring.

The Acclaim and the co-operative programme known as Project XX led to Rover's rehabilitation. It began in earnest in 1986 with the introduction of the 800, and was absolute by the 1990s, following the second generation of the 200 and the 400.

The model range once again divided into three distinct strains. If the 800 could be said to be the spiritual heir of the Rover Eighteens and Twenties of yore, and the inherited Metro a modern Rover Ten, the new 200 and 400 were the reincarnation of Rover Twelves and Fourteens. The designations were straightforward. The first digit was the model number, the other two referred to the engine size. Thus 213 was 200-series, 1.3-litre, and so on.

It was perhaps the reliability of the Rover 200 that affirmed its appeal to Rover's traditional middle-class market. Smooth-running and quiet, it was furnished with handsome polished woodwork and, for those who wanted to pay more, quality leather.

Yet if the first 213s and 216s were much the same as Hondas, their successors were not. Rover's growing self-confidence asserted itself with four British designed and made versions of

K-series engine had long through-bolts holding aluminium sandwich together.
(left)

the replacement Honda Concerto. A trend that became apparent in the 1930s, and then the 1940s, was repeated once again in the 1980s. A demand for smaller cars was always evident in harsh economic times. The jargon term was 'down-sizing'.

Demographic changes obliged former company car drivers to become private owners, perhaps for the first time. Higher fuel costs and worries about pollution encouraged the tendency, and Rover was ready with the answer.

A lot of customers, seeing the sense of compact cars, were still reluctant to give up the luxury and refinement of their Jaguar or BMW. They were by no means unhappy at the wheel of something smaller, but they were unwilling to relinquish the large-car characteristics to which they had grown accustomed. Former SD1 owners treasured the quietness and the smooth-running engine, and were not minded to give them up.

In October 1989 Rover gave them the new 200, a five-door hatchback series of cars that were smooth-running and quiet, resplendent inside with good materials and well-detailed fittings. The typical down-sizer need not even give up the element of prestige - the car was still a Rover.

Yet its most important constituent was not the fine furnishings, it was the K-Series engine. This was not a Honda.

It marked Rover's return to the self-sustaining world of car manufacture, with a novel form of engine construction nobody had used before.

In the final quarter of the 20th century it was not easy to come up with something new in automotive engineering. New engines were not like new cars. They became so expensive to design, build, and tool up for, that sometimes it was decades before they were replaced.

The Metro engine went back to 1949, and it still had some way to go in the 1980s, despite being noisy and a bit faint-hearted. It was created as an 803cc four-cylinder for the Austin A30, then went into the Morris Minor II in 1952. It was turned through 90 degrees and fitted in the Mini for 1959, and reappeared in the Metro in 1980. Its pushrod overhead valves represented some progress over side valves and it survived into the era of four-valve heads and belt-driven overhead camshafts, but only because BMC and British Leyland lacked the cash to develop replacements.

Rover had to find some £200 million to build a new plant for the K-Series, a family of engines expected to last well into the 21st century. They had to be ten per cent more economical, need less servicing, warm up faster, be lighter, more efficient, and meet all the exhaust emission regulations that could reasonably be anticipated.

Headlamp treatment on BS Coupé's jury-rigged bodywork. (above)

The novelty of the K-Series was conceived in 1984 by a team working under Roland Bertodo and including Stan Johnson. It was developed by Rover's head of powertrain engineering, Sivert Hiljemark, with a technique which met one of the main difficulties of making engines entirely in aluminium.

It embodied a principle that gained an international reputation and made Rover engineering a target for envious takeovers from commercial rivals the world over. The advantage of aluminium is light weight, the disadvantage is its cost. Yet an aluminium engine thick enough to be sufficiently strong is just about as heavy as a cast-iron one that is cheap. Rover engineers were well aware of the dilemma, for their aluminium ex-Buick V-8 exemplified it precisely.

It was light in weight, but General Motors replaced it with a cheaper iron engine as soon as it learned how to cast thin-walled cylinder blocks.

The key for the K was to build up the aluminium structure in layers, head, block, bearing housings and sump, and pull them together with ten 16in steel through-bolts. Each layer was matched carefully with the next, in an ingenious design as innovative as anything ever seen at a Tokyo motor show. The through-bolt construction was regarded by some engineers as a prototype of future engines made not

in aluminium but in ceramics or plastics.

There were three K engines at first, a 1.1 K8 of 1,120cc with one overhead camshaft, two valves per cylinder, and 60bhp with a carburettor. The 1.4 K8 was 1,397cc with 75bhp, and K16 was the same capacity with two overhead camshafts, four valves per cylinder, single point fuel injection and 95bhp.

The cylinder bore was 75mm; the differences were achieved by lengthening the stroke, the converse of the Wilks/Boyle '100mm' engine of the 1930s, which was increased in capacity by widening the bore. The K's overhead camshafts were driven by

a toothed belt which Rover claimed would last 100,000 miles. To prove it, prototypes were run for two million miles.

Customer, press, and trade approval for the economy and the refinement of the home-grown British K-Series was immediate. It was used for the 1.4-litre 214 model, and a 1.6 114bhp Honda was installed in the nimbler 1.6-litre 216. The middle of the car bore a clear resemblance to the Honda Concerto, the suspension was shared too, but the front and rear were distinctively different.

The new cars were 2.4in longer than those they replaced, a fraction wider,

but significantly the wheelbase was 4in longer to provide the rear-seat legroom their predecessors lacked. Anti-lock brakes and air-conditioning were optional.

The K16-engined cars were smoother and quieter. The higher-revving Honda had an urgent sound, while the 1.4 was relaxing to drive, with a top speed of around 105mph, which was probably fast enough for Rover Ten owners. The 1.6 would dash eagerly to 120mph or so, accelerating with the customary Honda verve. The K-Series provided 30 to 38mpg, the faster 1.6-litre, 28 to 35mpg. Both cars had crisp gearchanges and delightfully precise controls, with power steering an option on all but the most expensive models at an extra £330.

A fuel consumption of 40mpg was an achievable target, putting the cars among the top bracket in the class. The more powerful engine gave better acceleration (the 30-70mph sprint occupied 11sec) and better flexibility at low town speeds.

There was some engine hum on both versions. Noise invariably penetrated the passenger compartment from sideways-on engines, that sent more vibrations out sideways than end-on. Noise-deadening by foam that expanded inside the body cavities did a good job in suppressing road noise, giving the customers the feel of the high-quality medium-sized cars they

Racing in 1980s enhanced Rover's appeal to keen drivers. Victory in TT against BMW and Jaguar carried echoes of 1907. Tom Walkinshaw leads Win Percy at Monza. (left)

By 1985 SD1 front had more chrome. The special version of the Vitesse developed by Lotus included the front spoiler homologated for racing. 213 at rear shows shape of things to come. (right)

cherished. The structure lacked the bulk of a large car for sound-absorption, yet for a car 14ft 4in long and weighing under 2,500lbs it was uncommonly refined.

Eulogies on the new cars came quickly. Rover enjoyed a psychological advantage over its rivals when it came to press comment. It worked both ways. Throughout the dog days of the Leyland regime press criticism was fierce, especially over questions of reliability.

Came the dawn, and the emotional attachment readers had for Rovers was reflected in their handling by journalists. '*Rover returns to top of the class*' was a typical headline in *The Sunday Times*. *Autocar*'s cover proclaimed: '*Rover's new 200: good enough to be the best*'. Most people wanted Rover to succeed, and it was with delight that the new cars were commended, almost without reservation.

They were the closest since the P6 to Rover's traditional middle-class market. Smooth-running and quiet, they were furnished the way a Rover was expected to be. The decor was un-self-consciously arranged for the British market.

The wood trim was no longer solid West African walnut like the P5, but neither was it a photographic Formica reproduction like the P6.

Eagerly-awaited 800 had clean lines and good aerodynamics. Steadily improving quality later made it Britain's best selling executive car. (above)

There was a non-skid mat on the parcel shelf like the 2000 and SD1, so that something could be put down without it darting away when the car moved off. Rover was back to caring ways. Somebody was once again thinking of details. There was a fine tactile quality in the crisp gearchanging of the manual gearbox, the smoothness of the automatic transmission, the way the switches worked. David Bache's legacy survived. The manual gearbox was designed by Peugeot and modified and made by Rover at Longbridge, exemplifying the increasingly international nature of the motor industry.

The new generation of Rover designers, Roy Axe and Gordon Sked, had no need to fake the traditional old-style British car interior. They knew that wood and leather had a warmth that the British market preferred. They also knew it exported well. European markets in particular had grown to prefer the interiors used in Jaguars and Rolls-Royces, and strongly associated it with Rovers. Quality was exhibited in the tidy engine compartment, with no stray pipes or loose wires. It was shown in the tight body joins and the rust-inhibiting paint finishes.

When it came in 1990, the Rover 400 was like the 200, but with four doors and a boot. It had the same 1.4-litre and 1.6-litre engines, and the same high standard of finish and trim. Halving the engine capacity compared with the

SD1 did not halve the price. The four-door cars were costlier than the five-door versions with a slightly different model mix. The top 416 was the 125mph GTi with alloy wheels, leather upholstery, and electric sunroof included as standard.

Together the two new models achieved more than a change of heart. They won minds by design, particularly interior design, that struck a market keynote.

The mechanically similar Honda, the Concerto made at Longbridge, was efficient enough, but the inside was cheerless by comparison. The controls were light, the seats comfortable, although the ride remained capricious.

Fairly even and level on most roads, the car heaved itself uncomfortably over large bumps. The front-wheel drive gave safe, relaxed handling, and although it had no pretention about being sporty like the BMW, often claimed to be Rover's role model, it could be driven enjoyably quickly. The analogy with BMW became outdated. Rover was Rover's role model: Rover of the 1950s and 1960s, when the cars were middle-class, respectable, well made, quiet, and a turn of speed was almost incidental.

Rover began to inch its way towards a recovery of that essential Rover identity that some feared had been lost in the maelstrom of the 1970s. Sir Michael Edwardes forged the key, the

relationship with Honda: and the introduction of the Triumph Acclaim. Sir Graham Day and George Simpson now constructed the window of opportunity that Rover designers and engineers were able to open.

Besides the old Acclaim and 213 and 216, the new Rover largely replaced the unlamented Austin Maestro. It was the Austin name that was repudiated, not Rover. Poor Austin, consigned to the dustbin of history. The pioneering Austin Seven that saw off the Rover Eight in 1923 all but forgotten, the make that Betjeman mentioned in the same breath as Rover no more than a fragment of motor industry history.

In June 1986 the launch of the Rover 800 came after the Acclaim established the Honda connection, but before the relationship matured sufficiently to make the euphoria of the 200/400 possible. In 1986 it was still possible to contemplate each new Austin-Rover as a matter of the company's survival.

In the case of the 800, it was probably exactly that. Conceived and developed in a pioneering cross-world programme jointly with Honda, rather than simply made under licence like the Triumph Acclaim, the 800 replaced the ten-year old and somewhat unlamented SD1. It was important that Rover return to its traditional premium-priced product. It corresponded with Rover's name and reputation. It had the ring of logic

about it. This was the opportunity for Rover gratefully to leave the pursuit of numbers to others and concentrate once again on quality and prestige. It set out, in short, to regain its place as One of Britain's Fine Cars. It might have been tempted to use the time-honoured slogan over again save that it might have made itself a hostage to fortune, since it was soon to be 20 per cent owned by a Japanese company whose UK affiliate was in turn 20 per cent owned by Rover.

By the 800's launch in July 1986 only 1,500 cars were ready, all painted silver to speed up deliveries to 1,100 waiting dealers - production organisers had not learned many new tricks since their Edwardian forebears painted Rovers green. Some eager customers had to wait months. Production at Cowley was six months behind schedule, and Rover's sales target of 20,000 cars a year in Britain looked ambitious.

Most 800s - those at the cheaper end of the range - had their own Longbridge-built 2-litre engines. A descendent of the British Leyland O-Series, the M16 with twin belt-driven overhead camshafts powered the 820e and 820i. The upmarket versions, given the American-market name of Sterling, had Honda's 2.5 litre V-6, revealed in its own version of the car, the Legend, at the Tokyo motor show. The Legend and the 800 showed the way to changing the appearance of the smaller cars. The Rover lost the

Honda's sharply chiselled nose in favour of something closer to the superseded SD1.

There were three engine types, two 2-litres and one 2.5-litre V-6, all with four valves per cylinder, all with the same four-door body, all styled tidily rather than beautifully, but with a sophistication that put them among the best executive cars of the day. The Rover was no bland copy of the Honda Legend although it shared the floorpan, the inner body shell and the V-6 engine.

The 2-litre M16 was showered with praise for its good low-speed pulling power and economy. Its smoothness was compared favourably with the Japanese V-6 although its appearance was not. The V-6 had carefully arranged pipework and polished cam covers, the M16 a rougher-hewn demeanour. Rover learned, like Japanese motorcycle manufacturers, that taking trouble to finish an engine well on the outside suggested it was executed just as carefully on the inside.

The 800 was essentially European, and soaked up bumps rather better than its Japanese counterpart, except for a certain fidgetiness at slow speeds. As a front-wheel-drive car its handling was so self-possessed that comparisons were often drawn between Rovers and BMWs. It was meant to be a compliment. It would never have been seriously canvassed in the 1970s.

Rovers of 1907 and 1986.

(left)

Fine detailing returned
to Rover with the
non-skid mat in the
facia shelf.
(above)

Front-wheel drive made the 800
superbly predictable. Anti-lock brakes
were an option on the top models even
though Ford had standardised them on
the Granada. It may have looked like
Rover's reluctance to adopt hydraulic
brakes in the 1940s, but in a
competitive market the list price was
all powerful. There was even a short-
lived entry-level 820 with the old O-
Series engine from the Montego.

Top speed of the 2-litre was 125mph,
against well over 130mph for the V-6,
but it was a gentlemanly rather than a
racy car until the addition of the
Vitesse to the range. This was a name
inherited with Triumph, which applied

it to its 'speed' models of the Gloria
and Dolomite in the 1930s. It was
applied to the new Rover Fastback to
promote a racier image, and also to
counteract a buyers' hold-off in
France, where the hatchback SD1 had a
spirited following.

Prices edged upwards to match the
new status. A Vitesse that could touch
140mph and reach 60mph in 7.5sec
cost £20,443 without leather trim and
optional electrically adjustable seats.

It was pitched squarely against the
BMW 5-Series, Ford Scorpio, Saab
9000 and Alfa Romeo 164. It could
even be judged against the Mercedes-
Benz W124 and Jaguar range. No false
modesty here.

The Sterling failed, inexplicably, to
conquer America. It was launched
with high hopes in 1986, and deserved
to. Against a Cadillac Seville, which
retailed at about the same price, the
Sterling looked a certain winner.

The Cadillac's thirsty 4.1-litre V-8 felt
lumpish compared with the silken
V-6. The Cadillac had 132bhp to move
its 3,421lb body, the Rover 160bhp to
propel 200lb less. The Cadillac was less
nimble, the steering had little feel to it,
and the interior looked gaudy against
the Sterling's wood and leather, yet
America was not convinced.

The seven-year relationship between
Honda and Rover blossomed, although

Fastest production
Rover of its time,
Vitesse SD1 capable
of over 130mph.
(right)

it was not always plain sailing.
Honda's president, Tadashi Kume, said
at the launch of the 800 that despite
occasions *"where no resolution could
be reached"*, it had been *"truly
satisfying"*.

Rover owed less to Honda for the
820's success. Primacy for the car's
handling and roadholding lay firmly
in European hands, and with the
economical British four-cylinder it
was the best value of the range. At
£11,500 at launch time, it was also one
of the cheapest, with a smoothness and
refinement absent from Rovers for
too long.

But the management's employment of
its market research was imperfect.
When the 800 came out, the Sterling
was heavily promoted, with the result
that buyers imagined the whole range
more expensive than it was.

The strategy backfired. Rover was so
certain of the 800's superiority that it
was priced at Mercedes-Benz levels. It
was so much better made than
anything Rover had turned out in the
1970s that at £18,795 the Sterling
seemed, to the management at any rate,
to be going cheap.

The customers were perplexed. For a
time they overlooked the splendid
820e. It took time for it to recover the
ground lost in the 1970s and challenge
the Ford Granada for the title of
Britain's favourite executive car.

CHAPTER XII

Rover Nineties

As the 1990s approached, the Rover wheel came full-circle. The phases in its history when it became involved in mass-market cars were invariably less than happy. The Rover vision was always best placed when it lay at the quality end of the market. Spencer Wilks recognised it in the 1930s and discarded the Scarab. He acknowledged it again in the 1940s and abandoned the M-Type.

Rover was driven into the volume market through its relationship with British Leyland, and when that was dismembered it was left with an inheritance of Metros and Maestros and Montegos which, for all their assets, were not quite mainstream Rovers. It was not a question of size or speed; there had been plenty of small slow Rovers in its past.

There was no question of relinquishing this part of Rover's inheritance from the old regime. Instead the programme was adapted to Rover's changing posture. Spencer Wilks took over a moribund model policy in 1930; Sir

Graham Day was compelled to adapt what he took over to new circumstances in the 1970s and 1980s. Abandoning a successful small car like the Metro was not an option.

The Metro settled into the Rover fold. By the 1990s it had a Rover interior and a K-series engine, the quality was a match for anything, and it remained the world's best-packaged small car. Nothing put so much passenger room into so short a wheelbase. It was in every sense a worthy successor to the Rover Ten.

After over 1.5 million were made, a new engine, a five-speed gearbox, an improved driving position and better decor put the Metro back on the pedestal from which it had been knocked off by newer, more refined superminis such as the Peugeot 205 and the Ford Fiesta. Its nimble handling was unimpaired, the ride was smoothed by interconnected Hydragas springing, and the old transfer gear whine, a characteristic of gearbox-in-sump engines dating back thirty years to the Mini, was at last banished.

Fine leather, a Rover hallmark. (below)

Into the 1990s, a 200 Cabriolet. (right)

Graham Day joined the
Rover Group.
(above)

.... and so did the Metro.
(left)

Rover aimed to export one Metro in three to markets where it was known as the Rover 100. The Metro name lingered only in the UK, where loyalty to it persisted.

The five-speed gearbox was an option on the cheapest and in some ways the most effective Metro. The two-valve, 1.1-litre 60hp version replaced the old Metro City with a quiet, well-equipped small car, which was a delight to handle and promised

economy of between 40 and 50mpg.

The shape of the Metro did not change much. It was now slightly longer (by 118mm; 4.6in), the wheels moved closer to the front (by 19mm; 0.75in) and the front track was widened to accommodate the K-series engine. A few pressings such as the bonnet and tailgate were altered, and plastic mouldings round the bumpers and body sides transformed the appearance.

The interior was tidy and stylish, with the distinction of a comfortable driving position. The steering column was double-jointed to bring the wheel closer to the vertical.

In 1991 Rover reinstated its traditional radiator grille on the 800, to show it was once again making premium-priced quality cars. It rejoined BMW, Jaguar, Alfa Romeo, Mercedes-Benz and Lancia with stylised grilles, displaying once again a distinctive

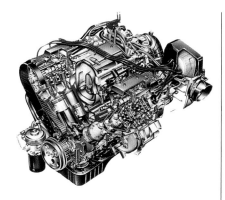

Modern masterpiece, the 24-valve 2.7-litre Rover 800 V-6 engine. (above)

Traditional radiator grille reinstalled on a Rover after nearly thirty years. The 1992 Sterling. (right)

feature in the executive car park.

The restyling only affected the front and back of the car. The designers were given a tight brief. Door pressings were expensive, so they had to make do with the same centre section and restyle the nose and tail. The new back was less successful than the front; its practical advantage was a bigger boot.

Pursuing niche markets continued with the introduction of cars such as the 800

Coupé, the T-series turbo Vitesse and a cabriolet version of the 200 in 1992. Rover took advantage of every opportunity, according to principles Spencer Wilks knew all about in 1938.

The 800 Coupé was a beautifully proportioned two-door version of the saloon, with the 2.7-litre V-6 engine and long flowing lines. The Hastings Coupé of 1933 set a style followed by many a Derby Bentley of 1936, when Rovers were known as poor men's

Bentleys only half in fun. They were often a match in speed and silence.

Bentley announced the Continental R at the Geneva motor show in 1991, and the Rover 800 Coupé - slightly smaller, a similar shape and a fifth of the price - followed the vogue for smart luxury two-door cars, at £30,770. It would have been good value £10,000 dearer, with leather upholstery, cruise control and air-conditioning. It was not as noiseless as a Lexus nor as swift as a

George Simpson,
managing director who
steered Rover into
the 1990s.
(above)

Flagship Rover Coupé.
(right)

Jaguar, but it was one of the best Rovers ever, with a matchless interior of hand-stitched leather and deeply polished wood.

It was slower than a 1990s Bentley at 130mph against 145mph, but none the worse for that. Yet it had something of the Bentley's grandeur and dignity, and was the first British car in the UK with a driver's side airbag.

No major manufacturer in the world produced such splendid interiors as Rover. It might have been better if the 800 Coupé's instrumentation and switchgear had broken new ground to make the best of the fine materials and finishes. Something better than the Sterling's old instrument panel would have been suitable.

The carpets were a deep, rich pile and the hand-stitched door casings furnished an aristocratic appearance. The seats were electrically adjusted, there was a fine-sounding Clarion Rover stereo with a compact disc player in the boot, automatic transmission, electric windows and central locking.

Bearing in mind some of the concept cars Rover showed, the Coupé was less sleek than expected. Typically it did not set trends, but kept up well enough for the doctors, lawyers and bank managers who formed Rover's traditional clientele not to feel left behind.

The transverse 2.7-litre V-6 engine driving the front wheels dated back to the Honda-Rover engine of 1986, and was as smooth as any of its rivals. It was a well-bred car, with reserves of speed and handling that made it surprisingly nimble, for 4.88 metres (16ft) long.

Rover filled another market niche with a rare four-seat open tourer, the 200 Cabriolet. It looked less of a styling success than the 800, owing to the cumbersome roll hoop necessary to restore the body strength sapped by removing the roof. The 1993 Rover 400 marked the return of the traditional radiator grille to the smaller cars with K and the renamed T-series engines, and the 418SLD diesel and 420 GSi sport turbo.

Dudley Noble's 1913 errand to meet Dr Diesel may have been abortive, but Rover's diesel cars of the 1990s proved highly successful. The Metro diesel with its Peugeot-derived engine was exemplary, providing a new role as an environmentally correct small car, with the extra mass at the front giving it an altogether more substantial feel entirely suitable to a Rover.

The 117mph, 36mpg 825 turbo-diesel was embraced by the press as '... *at last an executive diesel with the speed of a petrol counterpart*', and the 418SLD was a naturally aspirated compression-engined car for the businessman in the medium sector.

Synchro. Developed jointly with Honda, the 600 kept its traditional radiator shell and strong Rover identity with interiors designed by Gordon Sked. Engine balancer shafts invention of Edwardian engineer and philosopher Dr Fred Lanchester. (below)

Exteriors took on new lustre. (right)

Yet if the old Ten, Twelve and Fourteen had their modern counterparts, so also had the Speed Twenty and, in a sense Bache's favourite, 'Gladys'. The sporting derivatives Rover planned but somehow never brought to the market were realised at last in the 1990s.

The fastest Rover since JET 1 and the Rover-BRM was announced at the Paris motor show in 1992; the 200 Coupé Turbo was capable of 150mph. Characteristically it was not a fiery sports car. It was a gracefully understated fast touring car which, had it been the way of things in the closing years of the 20th Century, might well have challenged the Train Grand Vitesse (TGV) as Noble's Light Six did the Blue Train in the 1930s.

A traction control system brought technology to the aid of the driver, limiting wheelspin in the wet. The novel split glass roof was coated with titanium to keep the occupants cool in warm sunshine.

Rover remained Honda's foothold in Europe. With its manufacturing facility at South Marston near Swindon, Honda's relationship with Rover was crucial.

By the early 1990s the first of three joint ventures, code-named Synchro, was being produced in Swindon. The Honda version was the superbly refined Accord, a 2-litre and 2.3-litre four-door saloon; the Cowley-built Rover was distinctively styled with all the traditional features expected by buyers who inherited a Rover culture stretching back ninety years. Like the Accord, the new mid-range saloon attained levels of comfort and quietness that would have been the envy of more expensive peers half a generation ago.

Rover's span covered almost the entire history of the motor car. Yet from its tentative beginnings in the opening years of the 20th century to the dawn of the 21st, succeeding generations of engineers and designers and customers always managed to keep faith with an area of automotive endeavour that gave the world more than a brand-name. It provided an enduring legacy.